It's someone taking a part of you

A study of young women and sexual exploitation

Jenny J Pearce with Mary Williams and Cristina Galvin

GW00692052

JOSEPH
ROWNTREE
FOUNDATION

MIDDLESEX
UNIVERSITY

NSPCC
Cruelty to children must stop. FULL STOP.

NATIONAL
CHILDREN'S
BUREAU
making a difference

The National Children's Bureau promotes the interests and well-being of all children and young people across every aspect of their lives. NCB advocates the participation of children and young people in all matters affecting them. NCB challenges disadvantage in childhood.

NCB achieves its mission by
- ensuring the views of children and young people are listened to and taken into account at all times
- playing an active role in policy development and advocacy
- undertaking high quality research and work from an evidence based perspective
- promoting multidisciplinary, cross-agency partnerships
- identifying, developing and promoting good practice
- disseminating information to professionals, policy makers, parents and children and young people

NCB has adopted and works within the UN Convention on the Rights of the Child.

Several Councils and Fora are based at NCB and contribute significantly to the breadth of its influence. It also works in partnership with Children in Scotland and Children in Wales and other voluntary organisations concerned for children and their families.

The Joseph Rowntree Foundation has supported this project as part of its programme of research and innovative development projects, which it hopes will be of value to policy makers, practitioners and service users.

The views expressed in this book are those of the authors and not necessarily those of the National Children's Bureau, the Joseph Rowntree Foundation or Middlesex University.

Published by National Children's Bureau Enterprises Ltd, the trading company for the National Children's Bureau, Registered Charity number 258825. 8 Wakley Street, London EC1V 7QE. Tel: 020 7843 6000

© School of Social Sciences, Middlesex University, 2002
Published 2002

ISBN 1 900990 83 0

British Library Cataloguing in Publication Data
A catalogue record for this book is available from the British Library

Designed and typeset by Jeff Teader

Contents

List of tables

Acknowledgements

First and foremost, thanks are given to the 55 young women who took part in the research and whose case studies are referred to throughout. Thanks to *L*, aged 14, for her definition of sexual exploitation, *'It's someone taking a part of you'*, used as the title to this report. The direct quotations from the young women's narratives are deliberately intended to capture their own responses to everyday events. It is our commitment to ensure that energy is put into improving services in this area, to build on the dedication and enthusiasm that the young women themselves have given towards this action research work.

This project would not have been possible without the excellent work of the two research officers who developed case study material with the young women. Mary Williams was based in the Northern City as research officer from February 1999 to February 2002 and Cristina Galvin was based in the London Borough from February 1999 to November 2001. As is established, accessing and sustaining work with young people facing the difficulties described within the report can be stimulating and rewarding, but also dangerous, emotionally demanding, frustrating and sometimes deeply depressing (Melrose 2003 forthcoming). The significant quantity and depth of research material that was gathered is a testimony to their work.

Thanks also go to the NSPCC with whom a partnership arrangement was established to provide a professional practice context to the work. Nasima Patel, London based Project Manager and Permala Shemar, Project Manager for the Northern City location, both facilitated provision of premises, administrative support, ongoing staff supervision and consultation and provided a practice base for referrals for follow up work. Without this support the research work could not have taken place. Pat Cawson, Andy Haley and Peter Liver were particularly helpful during the early stages of establishing the work within NSPCC and Mitzi Wakefield played an instrumental role in facilitating future integration of the recommendations within NSPCC policy and practice. Donna Johnson of the NSPCC London Project tirelessly transcribed interview material, with support from Mavis Burke, Administrative Manager, and Carol Scarfe, NSPCC secretarial staff.

Thanks to the many local service delivery agencies in both locations who have provided consistent support to the work and who took time to complete an audit of local services. Specific thanks go to local project steering group members and to the working women's outreach service in the Northern City that supported the research officer in outreach, street based work. Nicola Mullenger worked imaginatively with project staff on the young women's photography projects. Inspector Chris Broome, Operational Head of the Street Offences and Juvenile Protection Unit of The Metropolitan Police Clubs and Vice Unit provided examples of good practice involving police work and gave access to useful data regarding young people taken into police protection in the Soho area of London. Margaret Rosemary, a consultant from a voluntary organisation from the Northern English City provided supervision on an ongoing basis.

The Tavistock Clinic of the Tavistock and Portman NHS Trust supported the work through provision of regular consultation sessions for the research team with Rose Golberg (Senior Clinical Lecturer in Social Work). Contact with Rose was invaluable not only for managing the research team's emotional responses to the work, but also for providing a context within which they could be understood. It was in these consultation sessions that many of the concepts and ideas developed within the report were founded.

Finally, thanks to the Joseph Rowntree Foundation and Middlesex University for funding and providing academic guidance to the work. The Foundation's emphasis on research support ensured invaluable project evaluation and progress reviews throughout the research. The Foundation's advisory group was an essential reference point, whose members provided informed and effective expertise to guide the work (see Appendix 1). As Chair of this advisory group, Charlie Lloyd's leadership and advice added significantly to the outcome of the study. His understanding of the difficulties involved in conducting the research enabled some of the more innovative research methods to be put into practice and he facilitated careful consideration of the data. Middlesex University also provided regular meetings with a Research Support Team. Led by Professor Susanne MacGregor, members of the team each contributed to the work. Professor MacGregor has given invaluable guidance throughout the duration of the project and, with Dr Betsy Thom, has advised on devising research methods and on managing the research process. Lynne Smith produced a thorough and detailed literature review. Malcolm Read worked on quantitative data with a speed and efficiency second to none and Ruth Turze helped work on data presentation.

Preface

Heroin: hurting lives, robbing wives

Feel the pain, feel the strain, feel the swelling of the brain.

Sitting down, walking round, wishing you were underground.

Knowing me, knowing you, wishing no one ever knew.

Drugs, shrugs and funny looks, cooking up, throwing up, giving up, cleaning up.

Laying down, coming down, feeling like a stupid clown.

Cold turkey, robbing an old lady. Little baby,

Big girl, bad girl, little girl, stupid girl.

No regrets, lots of debts, talking lots of stupid tests *.

Hurting lives, robbing wives, wondering why you should not die.

Feeling sorry, feeling low, feeling like you want a blow.

Locked up, knocked up, blocked up, cooked up.

Falling down, feeling down, looking around, spinning round,

Feeling like you're not worth a pound.

Wrong crowd, no longer proud, knowing this is not allowed.

Higher than a cloud, lower than the mud, never really thought about giving up.

Living dead in the red gouache, anywhere except for bed.

Walking, waiting, anticipating, never knew that you were breaking.

Want to go, want to stay,

don't know what today.

By 'F' (aged 14)

F confirmed that she meant talking, rather than taking, tests. She explained that she felt as though she was being tested when being asked to talk about her situation when in some meetings with professionals.

This report outlines the results of extensive case study work with 55 young women, aged 18 years and under, who are at risk of, or experiencing, sexual exploitation. The study was undertaken at two locations in the UK: a London Borough and a Northern City. Developed in partnership with the National Society for the Prevention of Cruelty to Children (NSPCC), the research aimed to gain young women's views about the choices and opportunities available to them during their transition to adulthood. The young women's language is used within the report as much as possible to reflect their descriptions of their experiences which, as will be seen, are invariably of exploitation, intimidation and violence. As a result, many of the terms used, such as 'boyfriend', 'swapping sex' or 'selling sex', must be understood within the context of abuse. It is this experience of abuse that often limits their scope to present other, more critical or objective descriptions of their circumstances. The poem, which prefaces this report, was written in response to the research project, by one of these young women. It highlights a number of the themes of the research: despite feeling trapped in circumstances that appear beyond their immediate control, these young women can also express profound insight about their predicament, employing courage and resilience as they seek to confront their situation.

These predicaments in which these young women find themselves can be so taxing as to put their own mental health in question. For example, S, aged 16, was referred for a psychiatric report after three years of frequent running from home and residential placements. Concern was expressed that she was getting into unknown men's cars, self harming through cutting herself and that she had an escalating problem of alcohol and heroin misuse, associated with her relationships with older men. However, the psychiatric report suggested that it was her circumstances, rather than her mental health, that were the problem. It confirmed that there were no biological features of depression or of clinically diagnosable mental health problems evident. Rather, S was reported as a 16-year-old struggling with a dysfunctional and abusive family history, which had provided her with little stability in her life. It was also noted that while she had emotional difficulties, she displayed some motivation to move forward and work towards becoming an independent and well functioning adult.

It is this sense of hope about moving forward that the report attempts to capture. For example, J, aged 17, ran from her home where her violent sister abused her, had a history of cutting herself for relief from emotional pain, had been raped whilst missing from home, and was engaging in 'risky' sexual behaviour with older men. Despite the difficulties facing her, she shows a strong drive for survival:

In a way I'm strong. I have to pick myself up and move on and
try to think of ways of making my life better and try to do the
things I've always wanted to do and make my dreams come true.
(J, aged 17)

For those working in this field, the material contained within this report will be
familiar. Many dedicated, knowledgeable and committed practitioners, researchers
and campaigners work with similar individual cases on an ongoing basis. It is hoped
that the findings presented here will help to enhance existing work and provide an
additional tool for those intending to raise the profile of the range of needs presented
by young women at risk of, or engaged with, sexual exploitation and prostitution.
While appreciating that the issues represented within this work affect young men as
well as young women (Barrett 1997, Palmer 2001), this research specifically built on
existing contacts made with projects targeted towards young women. It is hoped,
however, that the findings of this research can be used to open the investigation and
debate about all young people's experiences of sexual exploitation.

1. Themes from existing work

Introduction

This report draws on qualitative and quantitative findings from case study work undertaken in the United Kingdom with a total of 55 young women aged 18 and under: 25 from a Northern City and 30 from a London Borough. The young women were either at risk of or were currently being exploited through prostitution. The work aimed to provide the young women's own accounts of the choices and opportunities available to them in their transition to adulthood. As such, the research project was titled The Choice and Opportunity Project. It worked with young women on life story and case study work, using a range of individual case-work methods as well as photography, art and drama exercises.

The report provides a summary of the main findings from the research. Chapter 1 covers some of the themes emerging from existing research and project work that have been carried out within this area. It puts the research into context, explaining definitions and issues of concern identified by previous work. Chapter 2 then explains the aims and methods of The Choice and Opportunity Project, clarifying some of the ethical considerations for action research with young people exploited through prostitution. It provides an overview of the quantitative data drawn from the 55 case studies. Chapter 3 draws on young women's stories to identify the 'early signs' of risk for sexually exploited young women. Chapter 4 explores some of the issues facing young women who talk of 'swapping' sex when running away from home or care. It looks to their own accounts of how they became increasingly vulnerable to substance misuse and to abuse from exploitative adults. Chapter 5 looks to the reasons given by those young women who self define as prostitutes for starting and continuing to sell sex. It identifies the choices and opportunities facing them as they become increasingly dependent upon street based lifestyles. Finally, Chapter 6 identifies the main recommendations for policy and practice arising from analysis of the research findings.

Age of beginning to sell sex

Previous research has established that many women started selling sex when under 18 years of age as a result of poverty, abuse and exploitation (Barrett 1997, Pitts 1997). Melrose, Barrett and Brodie (1999) noted that 32 of a sample of 46 women and four men became involved with prostitution before the age of 16, 24 of whom started when they were 14 or younger. Pearce and Roache (1997) noted that of a sample of 43 women, 65 per cent were under the age of 17 when they started to sell sex. Barnard, Hart and Church (2002) noted that of a sample of 240 women selling sex, the mean age for entry to the work was 19 years old for those who worked outdoors, 63 per cent citing the need for money for drugs as the reason for having started. Although some adult women do make conscious, self determined decisions to work in the sex industry, research evidence argues that many start to sell sex when children, invariably poorly equipped to make informed choices about their future.

Issues of definition and the scale of the problem

Street based prostitution involving young people provides only a small, but visible, part of the 'bigger picture' of sexual exploitation of young people by adults. Even so, police data between 1989 and 1995, on cautions and convictions of young people for offences related to prostitution, show that a total of 2,380 cautions and 1,730 convictions were secured against those under 18 years of age in England and Wales (Aitchinson and O'Brien 1997). Behind these figures there remains an unknown number of young people who talk of selling or swapping sex for accommodation, drugs and other 'returns in kind', being increasingly vulnerable to manipulation by abusive adults.

Since 2000, innovative developments in practice have led to an acknowledgement that young people under the age of 18 years exploited through prostitution are victims of abuse, as opposed to perpetrators of crime. Agencies such as the police, social workers and other care and health professionals are now required to work together under local (welfare based) protocols enacted through the Area Child Protection Committees (ACPCs) (Department of Health 2000). Guidelines, issued by the Department of Health advise as to how the protocols should work to the dual aim of both protecting children and enabling the police to gather evidence about abusers and coercers (Department of Health 2000). The Department's guidelines state that:

> Children involved in prostitution should be treated primarily as
> the victims of abuse, and their needs require careful assessment.
> They are likely to be in need of welfare services and in many
> cases, protection under the Children Act 1989.
> *(Department of Health 2000, 3)*

Eighty-nine per cent of all ACPCs in England now have protocols in place, either
finalised or in draft form, and 51 per cent have established a sub-committee or
steering group to work with young people exploited through prostitution (Swann
and Balding 2002). Notwithstanding the remaining contradiction in law, that young
people under 18 years who persistently and voluntarily return to prostitution can still
be criminalised for offences related to prostitution, these amendments have
endorsed alternative ways of defining the problem. Since the changes, police data on
young people convicted of offences related to prostitution have dropped. However,
figures of young people under 18 years of age taken into police protection under
Section 46 of the Children Act 1989 continue to provide a 'tip of the iceberg' insight
into the scale of the problem. The London Metropolitan Police figures of the
Central London (Soho) area, for example, provide a helpful profile of young people
brought into police protection. Ninety-one young women were brought into police
protection on 255 different occasions in 1999, 48 being suspected of prostitution. A
further 55 young women were brought in suspected of prostitution on 101 different
occasions during 2000.

Of course, these figures only reveal those 'picked up' from the street by the police.
The review of the use of the Department's guidance (Department of Health 2000)
noted that 76 per cent of all ACPCs in England confirmed that there were children
involved in prostitution in their area, 28 from a targeted 50 ACPCs providing figures
showing a total of 602 children involved. Their findings suggested that there were an
average of 19 girls and three boys involved in prostitution in an area at any given time
(Swann and Balding 2002). Estimates from project work suggest that up to 5,000
young people are involved in prostitution in the UK at any one time (Crosby and
Barrett 1999). A survey of 48 agencies conducted by Barnardo's in 1998 reported
contact with more than 300 children under 16 years of age who did not necessarily
self define as 'prostitutes', but who were clipping (taking money from a punter and
then running without exchanging sex) and/or were selling or swapping sex for
money, drugs, accommodation or other good 'in kind' (van Meeuwen and Swann
1998). Our own audit within this research of a total of 21 local services from the
London Borough and the Northern City provided knowledge of 269 young women
aged 18 and under, 165 of whom were known to be exploited through prostitution.
The other 104 were not selling sex for money, but were swapping sex, being sexually

exploited. Of the 269 young women, 160 were known to have had experience of being 'looked after' under the Children Act 1989, and 89 were known to have problems with misuse of Class A drugs.

Undertaking our own audit illustrated the difficulties in collecting data when definitions, policy and practice amongst practitioners vary. For example, some agencies ensured total client confidentiality from research and/or other service providers, while others shared information and worked more closely with Social Services. Some agencies were knowledgeable of problems associated with substance misuse while others had less experience in identifying, and therefore working with the signs. Where different agencies had contact with the same young woman involved in sexual exploitation or prostitution, there were often wide discrepancies in the definitions used to describe the circumstances involved. The experience of undertaking the local audits re-enforced the need for a shared understanding of 'sexual exploitation' and for subsequent data collection regarding contact with young people so classified. While maintaining a focus on protecting children from abuse, the parallel aim of prosecuting the abusers should not be lost within this shared understanding, only 6 per cent of 50 targeted ACPCs currently believing that they are meeting the dual aim of protecting children and helping the police to gather evidence against abusers (Swann and Balding 2002).

The different definitions of sexual exploitation that are emerging place the concept of coercion as central to the understanding of exploitation. For example, the one used for this research is:

> Any activity containing or suggesting a sexual component that a
> person is not consenting to freely, that it contains varying
> degrees of coercion that could vary from gentle persuasion to
> intimidation or violence.
> *(NSPCC project)*

while another, originally developed by Manchester ACPC (cited in Calder 2001) also introduces the notion of exchange, a feature prevalent within many of the case studies of the young women who took part in this research:

> A form of sexual exploitation rationalised by the concept of
> exchange. It is specifically exploitation of young men and women
> where they have needs that would compromise their ability to
> provide any form of informed consent to such activity. Exchange
> can be used to describe both tangible (money, drink, drugs) and
> intangible (shelter, protection, coercion) forms of payment.

Running from home or care

Existing research suggests that young women who run away or go missing can come from a range of different social classes and racial backgrounds, and that a 'running career' develops over time (Patel 1994, Kirby 1995, Wade and Barnett 1999, Safe on the Street Research Team 1999). The Children's Society notes that approximately 100,000 children have run from home or care in one year, more than 100 children running from home each day (www.childrenssociety.org.uk). Comprehensive research on young runaways carried out by the Home Office noted that one fifth of the respondents argued that they were 'forced' to leave home, implying that even if they wanted to return, they would not be welcome (Home Office 2001). Refuge provision for young people running from home is sparse. The one refuge for children under 16 years of age in the country is based in London and run by the NSPCC. It has eight beds and provides accommodation for two weeks. During the period April 2001 to February 2002 there were 387 referrals to the refuge with 122 admissions involving 97 young people, 84 of whom were young people referred for the first time. Fifty-seven of the non-admissions were because no beds were available at the time of referral. Of those admitted, 56 young people said that they ran from home or care because of arguments and conflict, 22 saying that they had been told to leave home, and therefore felt unable to return. Inevitably there is complicated casework between young people and their carers, and because of the two-week turn around period, negotiations have to take place over relatively short time spans (London Refuge 2002).

If the running career evolves so that the young person moves from their immediate area into an unfamiliar city, they become increasingly vulnerable to exploitation and violence. While girls can experience a range of different forms of violence in both public and private places (Burman, Tisdall and Batchelor 2002), movement into an unfamiliar area means that previous coping mechanisms, based on local knowledge, become undermined (Pearce and Stanko 2000, Alder and Worrall 2003 forthcoming). Many young people who run from care have few financial resources, and their marginalised position then becomes exacerbated through poverty (Davis 1997). Centrepoint, a central London charity for homeless young people, notes that 39 per cent of those children under 16 years of age who used their services had no income or money of their own, a further 48 per cent having up to £39 to their name (Centrepoint 1997, 6). The combination of poverty, familial abuse, drug misuse and social exclusion/marginalisation places young people running from home in specifically vulnerable conditions. With few, if any, personal or financial resources for support, they are highly susceptible to exploitation (Pitts 1997, Crosby and Barrett 1999, Noell and others 2001).

Coercion by abusive adults

It has been argued that abusive adults can use the concept of exchange, or swapping, to coerce young people into prostitution. Invariably, although not always, the abuser will target young people who have run away from home, often from familial sexual and physical abuse (Barrett 1997, Shaw and others 1996, Dodsworth 2000). A government consultation document highlights the vulnerability of those who runaway; 25 per cent of their sample slept rough and survived through stealing, small-scale drug dealing and prostitution (Home Office 2001). Many young women who are sexually exploited or who are selling sex have little existing contact with the education system and are marginalised from most other mainstream provision (Zigman 1999). This background of abuse and isolation makes young people easy prey for adults with sophisticated methods of coercion and manipulation for their own gain (Shaw and Butler 1998, Ivison 1998, Dodswoth 2000, Melrose, Barrett and Brodie 1999). The methods of exploitation are illustrated well in the video 'Whose Daughter Next' (van Meeuwen and Swann 1998), which gives a helpful insight into the means by which young people can be manipulated and exploited through coercion by an older adult, usually a man, who poses as a 'boyfriend'. The adult male grooms the young woman for prostitution as she falls in love with, and becomes dependent, upon him. He does this through three stages: (a) fantasy, (b) grooming, then (c) abuse. During the fantasy stage he entices her to believe that he loves her and that he will care for her, increasingly leading her away from her familial/care and peer networks. He then grooms her into sexual activity, often increasing her dependence upon drugs while so doing. Finally he introduces her to prostitution. As a result, the young woman is dependent both upon the abusive male, who can then become her pimp, and upon drugs. At a psychological level, any previous experiences of violence and abuse within interpersonal relationships have been confirmed, and her self-esteem, temporarily raised through the fantasy stage, is lowered further than before.

Barnardo's notes that, of girls seen by their projects since 1995, those aged between 12 and 14 did not make their own decision to sell sex, but were coerced by a man aged 18 to 25 (www.Barnardos.org.uk). While many young women coerced into prostitution may have previous experiences of abuse, it is not to be assumed that sophisticated abusers cannot manipulate children from a variety of previous background experiences. Case histories have illustrated how the self-esteem of a young woman can be destroyed through manipulation, irrespective of her past confidence in self (Broadfoot 1998). While acknowledging that poverty and previous experiences of abuse can make young women more vulnerable to manipulation,

Ivison broadens the profile to include children from a range of social backgrounds (Ivison 1998). This work, as well as helpful training material on abuse and exploitation available through many of the children's charities, explores all young people's potential vulnerability to abusive relationships with adults, highlighting that coercion is one of the many ways through which young people find themselves in prostitution (www.Barnardos.org.uk, www.nspcc.org.uk, www.childrenssociety.org.uk).

Substance misuse and sexual exploitation

Drug use, including heroin, crack cocaine, cannabis and serious alcohol misuse, are also widespread among young runaways and those vulnerable to exploitation (Green, Day and Ward 1999, Ward and others 2000). There is a complicated relationship between sexual exploitation, substance misuse, violence and prostitution (Phoenix 1999, Scrambler and Scrambler 1997), with different patterns of drug consumption among the various settings (Barnard, Hart and Church 2002). Crack use amongst London prostitutes was found to be increasing and was associated with multiple health problems including unwanted pregnancies, STIs and homelessness. Women selling sex and using crack were more likely to use the streets, to inject drugs and have a partner who injected (Green, Day and Ward 1999, Ward and others 2000). However, in line with the findings from the current study (see Chapter 5), Cusick found that no simple causal link between prostitution and drug use can be drawn (Cusick 1998). The relationship is therefore a complex one, a number of coexisting factors contributing to reasons for young people starting to sell sex (Crosby and Barrett 1999).

Jarvis, Copeland and Walton (1998) have argued that adolescence is a critical time for interventions around drug misuse, proposing that these interventions need to concentrate on issues of self-esteem and self worth amongst young people. There is evidence that the age of first use is declining (Parker and others 1995, 1998), suggesting that interventions should target young people in early adolescence. The 1998 Youth Lifestyles Survey highlighted drug use amongst vulnerable young people, and reported that half of all truants, as well as those excluded from school, reported using illicit drugs compared to 13 per cent of all school children. Seven per cent of those excluded from school were found to be using Class A drugs regularly, with drug use being higher for young women than young men. Four out of five rough sleepers had tried an illicit drug and 80 per cent of serial runaways were using illicit drugs (Goulden and Sondhi 2000). Despite this high level of use, there is a dearth of residential drug rehabilitation centres specifically targeted towards adolescents within the UK. Middlegate Lodge, currently the only such provision, employs a multidisciplinary team to provide a 12-week residential treatment service for adolescents experiencing substance misuse (Middlegate Lodge 2002). There is increasing onus on the development of comprehensive education about the prevention of substance abuse, drug awareness, harm prevention and minimisation overall. This is appropriate, but needs to be supported by a comprehensive programme of treatment for those young people who do already have problems with addiction. Despite new guidelines put forward in 1998 by the Standing Conference of Drug Abuse and The Children's Legal Centre identifying key principles to ensure that young people receive appropriate care, there remains very limited provision of local resources targeted specifically towards the treatment of problem substance abuse amongst young people. As noted by Drugscope 'most drug services are only equipped to deal with adult users' (www.drugscope.org.uk).

Violence and sexual exploitation

Work carried out through the ESRC Violence Programme confirms high levels of unreported violence experienced by young and adult women, many of whom do not disclose the harassment, abuse and violence to support agencies (Stanko, O'Beirne and Zaffuto 2002). One of the key findings from recent research by Barnard, Hart and Church (2002) was that while two thirds of 240 women selling sex reported violence from clients, only one third had ever reported violence to the police. Street sex workers reported most violence, being slapped, kicked or punched, 28 per cent reporting either vaginal, or anal, rape. The results of this research also showed that, in the main, it was the younger women found working on the streets, those inexperienced in developing defences against abuse from punters, who were most vulnerable to violence. Melrose, Barrett and Brodie (1999) undertook a retrospective study into the circumstances of 50 women working as prostitutes which revealed that many had moved from experiences of violence at home to violence at work. Thirty-six of the 50 women interviewed reported experiences of conflict and abuse in their families of origin, 21 noting their first sexual experience to be in the context of abuse. Amongst others, children's charities such as The Children's Society, Barnardo's and the NSPCC, have pioneered both project work and research to identify and meet the needs of some young people experiencing violent coercive relationships. Conferences such as 'Hidden Children, Child Prostitution – finding London Solutions' (2000), and 'Still Running: Children on the street in the UK' (1999) and training material available through the websites of the above organisations, identify the violence associated with the exploitation of young people. However, as explored in Chapters 3 to 5, the nature of the relationship between violence and coercion of young people is complex, and would benefit from further research and understanding for the development of informed service delivery.

Policy and practice

Swann and Balding (2002) have provided a wide ranging survey of the effectiveness of the local protocols for working with children involved with sexual exploitation and prostitution by Area Child Protection Committees. This work confirms that the Area Child Protection Committee (ACPC) is the appropriate lead body to develop interventions supporting young people exploited through prostitution and that explicit criteria for evaluation of practice should be developed. In line with the arguments made by Dodsworth (2000), the work proposes that additional resources are needed to ensure a holistic approach to the problem, connecting the work of local outreach voluntary services with statutory provision, and ensuring that comprehensive training is provided to practitioners from a range of services. There is now also a general recognition of the importance of identifying the abuser as a means of protecting young people (Ayre and Barrett 2000, Shaw and Butler 1998, Swann and Balding 2002). Outlining the legislation that can be used against pimping, Benjamin Nolan QC (Nolan 1998, 18) notes that some of the most common problems encountered in prosecuting the pimp are:

- witness intimidation;
- witness's fear of the pimp, resulting in reluctance to make a statement or to continue with proceedings;
- finding and keeping in touch with the witness.

Similarly the police and associated services must face the dilemma that gathering evidence means surveying the perpetrator enticing and coercing the young woman, placing her at further risk during the process of intelligence gathering. Without the young women being able or prepared to collaborate in providing evidence and pressing charges, it has been difficult for cases against abusers to be made. Attempts to address some of these problems have been made in The Netherlands where prosecution of the abuser does not have to rely upon a complaint being made by the young person themselves. The legislation notes that minors (children under 18 years of age) cannot be criminalised for offences relating to prostitution and abolishes the 'complaint requirement' for sexual acts involving children under 16 years of age. It is hoped that the abolition of the complaint requirement will enable 'child prostitution and sex tourism to be tackled more effectively' (voorlichting@ best-dep.minjust.nl 01.07.97 in Pearce 2000). This is referred to again in Chapter 6.

These progressive developments should be explored in framing legislation targeted at prosecuting those who exploit young people through prostitution. In the interim, Firth (1998) argues that the way forward is through inter-agency work that supports the young person throughout the process of prosecution of the offender. Essentially this means first recognising that the tactics used by the pimp (boyfriend) are comparable to those used by paedophiles, and then ensuring that once the child is away from immediate harm, ongoing liaison between police, social services and other related agencies takes place. Firth draws on findings of a project undertaken in Wolverhampton between August 1997 and February 1998, which involved coordinated and dedicated multi-agency work between police, social work and voluntary agencies. Out of 40 children involved with a pilot scheme, 11 were prepared to act as witnesses against their abusers, leading to nine adults being charged of serious offences, including rape, unlawful sexual intercourse, kidnapping, false imprisonment, assault and living off immoral earnings. The Child Abduction Act 1984, Section 49 of the Children Act 1989 (relating to abduction of a child) and Section 50 of the Children Act 1989 (relating to recovery of a child) provide some of the specific elements of legislation to be considered in prosecuting abusive adults who may incite a young person to run from care or from the designated responsible adult.

In the current White Paper, *Protecting the Public* (Home Office, 2002) the Home Office recognises that we need specific offences relating to the sexual exploitation of children. The White Paper proposes that it should be an offence to encourage a child into commercial sexual exploitation or facilitate the commercial sexual exploitation of a child. The White Paper also notes that 'procuring a child under the age of 16 for sexual activity will be covered by criminal law even if no commercial motive is involved'. While this is welcomed and encouraged, the question of how credible evidence is gathered to bring a case against an alleged offender, without placing the child further at risk, remains in need of further consideration.

Conclusion

This chapter aims to have covered some of the issues that have been raised by previous project work and research relating to young people involved with sexual exploitation and prostitution. The key themes identified within the chapter highlight the need for a focused inter-agency strategy on supporting young people vulnerable to entry to sexual exploitation and prostitution. This includes the need for a common, shared understanding of what constitutes sexual exploitation so that different agencies can collect consistent data on young people to provide some indication of the scale and prevalence of the associated problems. There is a clear need for fast track, targeted work to support young people at the early stages of their running away 'careers'. In the complicated tangle of overlapping causes and affects between drug and alcohol misuse and vulnerability to exploitation from abusive adults, this needs to involve coordinated inter-agency work, a point developed further in Chapter 6. Finally, there is the potential to expand the scope offered by current legislation to protect young people from abuse and to press charges against those abusing them. Chapter 6 continues this debate, identifying recommendations for future practice. Before looking at the findings explained in Chapters 3 to 5, the research methods and associated ethical considerations are explored in more detail in Chapter 2.

2. Research aims, methods and quantitative data

Introduction

This chapter explains the original aims of the research, the methods used and descriptive information employed to address the associated ethical considerations. The research methods employed in the study were designed to engage young women with 'life story case study work' and to consult with them on an ongoing basis about the progress and findings of the research. In following these aims, a number of important ethical considerations arose. For example, concerns about confidentiality had to be addressed with the young women. It was also important to consider their responses to being asked to confront issues in their lives that could be deeply upsetting. The chapter also outlines the issues involved with gaining access to young women, who were often invisible to mainstream service providers. There were also questions of 'labelling' to be confronted, as well as how to ensure that the data being collected was credible and reliable. The chapter then identifies the main themes that arose from analysis of the quantitative data from the 55 young women who took part in the research.

Aims

First and foremost, The Choice and Opportunity Project aimed to provide child centred perspectives of the problems and dangers associated with sexual exploitation and prostitution. To ensure that the survey included a full spectrum of those at risk, the work aimed to contact those hidden within exploitative relationships as well as those more visibly involved with street based prostitution. This meant engaging with both outreach, street based work and with drop in, project based networking, encouraging the 'snowballing' of information about the research: the process whereby young people spread information about the research and recruited others to take part themselves. As an action research project, the aims included a specific focus on working with local service providers, informing them of the findings and consulting them about the development of appropriate service delivery for this client group. To this end, the findings have been discussed by local, multi-professional steering groups.

The two locations where the research took place

The two locations were selected to provide comparison between an inner London borough and a northern city, both of which had a history of research with young and adult women working in prostitution. They provided a basis for contrast between a northern city, which had been an active centre for coal-mining, undergoing a process of urban regeneration and an inner London borough which had experienced an intensive programme of urban regeneration during the 1990s. The London Borough was the poorest of all London boroughs (London Borough: Crime and Disorder Audit 1999). However, as a result of the regeneration programmes, it had expensive, privately owned accommodation used by those working in the City of London which were placed in close proximity to deprived and poorly resourced social housing estates. Similarly, one third of the wards of the Northern City were among the most deprived 104 of all wards in England whilst two were among the least deprived. Despite these similarities, differences existed between the two locations in the age range, racial origins and density of the populations. Thirty-three per cent of the 179,834 population in the London Borough were from minority ethnic groups, compared to 5 per cent of the 530,000 population of the Northern City. Twenty-five per cent of the population of the London Borough were aged 16 to 24, whilst the largest age group in the Northern City was of those aged 35 to 39, although an influx of approximately 35,000 students each year introduce an increase in the numbers of young adults aged 20 to 24 (Northern City: Crime Reduction Strategy). Under the crime prevention strategies developed under the Crime and Disorder Act 1998, both locations recognise street based prostitution to be a problem, the London Borough noting that there are 'a small number of prostitutes operating in the area under the age of 17' (London Borough: Crime and Disorder Audit 1999, 22). The latter explores ways that the council, police and support agencies can address the problems arising, including targeting clients for arrest and offering support to prostitutes to deal with their problems.

The nature of the partnership with the NSPCC in the two different locations

In recognition of the emotional and psychological demands placed upon young women and researchers through the process of engaging with research of this nature, the project worked in partnership with the NSPCC to ensure that

(a) a referral point was available if a young woman contacted was deemed to be at risk of 'extreme and immediate danger', or if confidentiality had to be breached for the welfare of the child;

(b) research workers could access regular supervision, support and professional expertise whilst engaging with difficult and potentially dangerous cases and situations;

(c) there would be a follow up in future service delivery aimed towards the prevention of sexual exploitation and prostitution of children.

In the London Borough the research officer was attached to a specific NSPCC project designed to work with young women deemed to be at risk of sexual exploitation and prostitution.

In the Northern City the officer was attached to an NSPCC project which provided a full range of services for young people, giving scope for specialist work with targeted groups if and when appropriate. As young women at risk of, or exploited through, prostitution can be difficult to work with (presenting behaviour that can fluctuate between running away from contact, aggressive rejection of support to making immediate demands for assistance), the support from NSPCC project staff was essential. Each research officer was based within the NSPCC premises, using the facilities for meeting with young women and/or associated workers. The researchers attended relevant staff and referral meetings. In the main, the case study research work with the young women took place independently from NSPCC project staff unless issues of confidentiality meant that additional contact was advised. The NSPCC staff maintained a supportive role to the research, being available for consultation on professional and ethical considerations where appropriate. Individual interviews with NSPCC staff, practitioners from other local agencies such as outreach projects, police, education and social services were undertaken by the researchers to help extend their understanding of local politics and policies for working with the client group.

Methods

Child centred research

The research was child centred, aiming to reveal the young women's perspectives on their own stories and giving them the opportunity to comment on the process and findings of the research. Researchers engaged with the young women through case study work over an 18-month period. This involved regular meetings with young women, most of which took place on a one-to-one basis and often needed extensive organisation in advance, facilitating journeys to and from the meetings. Instead of following a prescribed pattern of ongoing work, the meetings often responded to an immediate crisis as presented by the young woman. Throughout, case study work involved the development of a working relationship with the young women, undertaking life story work, looking both into the past and future to identify the choices and opportunities available to them. Young women were encouraged to draw life story maps, to write stories, poems and letters, taking photographs and doing art work to illustrate their circumstances and feelings. They were encouraged to keep confidential diaries from which they could select material for discussion. Wherever agreed between researcher and young women, conversations were tape recorded and transcribed to be used for the research. Researchers also maintained regularly updated research diaries. These provided an important source of information about the issues the young women were facing and the researchers' feelings that were generated by doing the work. A service agreement was written between The Choice and Opportunity Research Project and the NSPCC to cover issues of confidentiality and use of material for the purpose of research.

Group work and activity based projects

The case study work was predominantly carried out on a one-to-one basis. However, where drop-in facilities were available, the researcher would act as a participant observer, helping project staff and recording their own observations in their researcher's diary. Similarly, art work was carried out with young women on their own, or in pairs. Activities included drawing pictures, making face masks and wearing fancy dress. Each of these activities served to prompt discussion and provide a context within which the young women felt able to talk (for further information about the use of art work within similar research, see O'Neill, Campbell and Webster 2002). This approach used by The Choice and Opportunity Project argues that process can be as important as outcome: that the learning and experience gained for those working with the research can be as important as the findings that emerge.

Photography project

The research team also undertook a photography project with the young women, each of whom were given disposable cameras and asked to take pictures of whatever they felt important. Many of the young women found it a novelty to have a camera, being excited about being given both the responsibility to take their own pictures and the means to do so. In one of the locations the photography project took place at the time that the researcher was on leave. There was concern that, unsupervised, the young women would lose the cameras or discard them, but instead, on her return she discovered they had each taken and arranged a portfolio of pictures. The young women were given the opportunity to take photographs away with them and/or to select one to be transposed onto teeshirts that they kept for themselves.

Ethical considerations

Confidentiality

The purpose of the research was fully explained to the young women who participated and they were made aware that their case study material would only be used with their identity protected. Asking young people to disclose their experiences of abuse and exploitation had the potential to reveal unexplored areas of concern for the young women and disclose information that, under the Children Act 1989, is deemed to place the young person at risk of 'significant harm'. This presented an ethical dilemma. While such information should be referred on to statutory child protection workers, there was concern that young women might not disclose valuable and important information if they feared a breach of confidentiality.

To solve this problem the research project offered confidentiality to the young women apart from in 'exceptional circumstances', defined as 'in extreme and immediate danger'. The work referred to a checklist of what was understood by extreme danger and where necessary researchers discussed any dilemmas they felt about its application under the Children Act 1989 with NSPCC staff. The threshold for the confidentiality policy was agreed by the local Area Child Protection Committees (ACPCs) and by the NSPCC. As noted above, the partnership arrangement with the NSPCC ensured that, if required, follow up contact and support could be offered to all the young women contacted in the study.

Accessing 'hidden populations'

This research shows, as evidenced elsewhere, that while sexual exploitation is relevant to young women from a variety of different racial origins, it is mainly white young women who are more visible as street workers (McKeganey and Barnard 1996). To counter this bias, every effort in both locations was made to access the range of settings where young women might be sexually exploited, swapping or selling sex. As far as possible, all relevant agencies that had contact with young women from a range of racial, social and cultural backgrounds were approached.

All 55 young women held British passports. Three of the 55 young women had entered the country when children, having witnessed and experienced violence, rape and murder associated with war in their home country of origin. The other young women were from families who had, for a minimum of one generation, lived in, or close to, the immediate areas where the research took place.

Work with young women of Asian origin who were referred to the London NSPCC project raised a number of questions. NSPCC staff and researchers questioned whether different expectations of sexual activity were being applied to Asian and white young women. Asian young women, were, in particular, found to be referred at earlier stages of risk of sexual exploitation than their white counterparts. The referral was invariably appropriate, but concern was expressed that similar identification of the 'early warning signs' discussed further in Chapter 3 were not being identified for white young women so quickly. It became apparent that questions about the rationale for referral needed to be reviewed on an ongoing basis.

The research also recognised that while women may be selling sex to men, it cannot be assumed that they do not have intimate and/or sexual relationships with women (McKeganey and Barnard 1996). It was deemed important for the research to be open to talk that embraced both positive and negative sexual and emotional experiences with men and women. The research team were sensitive to the notion of forced heterosexuality and appreciated that, as a period of transition, adolescence will raise questions for young women both about their own sexual orientation and the quality of their relationships with men and women. For this reason full scope was provided in interview, discussion and case work for young women to recognise the importance of their different emotional and sexual relationships.

Labelling

Prior to and throughout the course of the research, some practitioners expressed concern that identifying and working with a young woman vulnerable to sexual exploitation could lead to them being labelled as potential prostitutes. Not only did some practitioners want to protect the young woman from being thus labelled, but it was also felt that for their own safety, those who were selling sex should be protected from identification. This concern is not to be taken lightly, as prejudice, contempt and violence have been directed towards women selling sex on the street, reflected in vigilante attacks, harassment and murder. For black and minority ethnic young and adult women the sexual harassment and violence can be compounded by racial violence (Kinnell 1999).

The research provided three responses to these concerns.

Young women's voices: Practitioners were assured that the work with young women focused on gaining the young women's definitions of their circumstances. This central priority meant that the young women themselves would be given the opportunity to provide meaning to the different ways that they describe themselves. The report maintains this focus, providing the young women's voice throughout.

Protecting safety: The safety of the young women who took part in the research was given the highest priority at all stages. To this end the specific locations where the research took place are not provided. Travel arrangements were discussed with each young woman prior to meetings taking place. It was common for the research officers to walk the young woman to her bus stop or tube station and to maintain some form of contact until she arrived safely at her destination. Interviews on the street were conducted only if the safety of the young woman was not threatened. Some fruitful interviews were postponed or cancelled if it appeared that attention was attracted to the young woman or if punters/boyfriends were suspicious. A close working relationship with local police was maintained so that communication about possible threats of local unrest could be maintained.

Protecting identity: The young women's identity is protected through the use of initials throughout the report. The details of the young women's cases are accurate to the circumstances that she described in her casework. If it appeared that too much information could reveal the young woman's identity, it has been withheld. The use of initials, rather than substitute names intends to hide the racial origin of the young women. Concern was expressed that identifying racial origin may lead to false assumptions of behaviour attributed to cultural difference. While work was carried out with black young women to address their experiences of racism, it was evident that all young women, both black and white, were vulnerable to sexual exploitation, coercion and violence from within the home and outside.

Further considerations regarding ethical considerations ('accessing credible data' and 'researcher's supervision and support') are explored in Appendices 2 and 3.

The central story from analysis of quantitative data

The following quantitative data gives an overview of the issues facing the 55 young women who took part in the case study work. This information was gained through the techniques explained above as well as through consultation with previous case file notes where appropriate and available.

Sample numbers

A total of 55 young women were involved in the study, 30 in the London Borough and 25 in the Northern City. The slightly larger group of young women in London was because the local NSPCC project was specifically designed to target young women at risk of sexual exploitation, having more designated staff resources for back up service delivery if needed to support the research work. The NSPCC project in the Northern City provided a generic service for a range of young people, and therefore had less direct contact itself with this particular client group.

Table 2.1 How contact was made with the 55 young women

19	Outreach work on the street (self referred)
8	Self-referred or attended the drop in with a friend
14	Social work
7	Schools and related education department services (Education Social Work and Pupil Referral Units)
4	Local women's projects: outreach services/domestic violence projects
1	Homeless Persons Unit
1	Social Work and Health Project: Child and Family Consultation
1	Referred by Youth Offending team

Table 2.1 shows that 27 young women were contacted through the research without prior referral from an existing agency. Nineteen of the 27 young women were contacted through street based outreach work. This involved researchers contacting young women on the street, usually late at night. Researchers accompanied NSPCC staff or other local outreach projects on street based outreach sessions. The further eight young women self-referred by attending the NSPCC project based 'drop in' facility, either on their own or with a friend. Six of these eight young women who made contact via self-referral or through attending drop in facilities with a friend were from the London based project work. This was because the London Project ran its own drop in facility specifically for young women, which increasingly attracted self-referrals and contacts through friendship groups. Apart from this difference, contact with young women from the two different locations followed a similar pattern, providing access to young women who were already known by service providers as well as with those who had little, if any, contact with other professional support.

Table 2.2 Age of young women by location

Age	London Borough n=30	Northern City n=25	Total n=55
13	2	1	3
14	6	7	13
15	3	3	6
16	7	6	13
17	8	6	14
18	4	2	6
Mean age	15.8	15.6	15.7

Table 2.2 shows that the sample contained similar numbers of young women from each age group in both the Northern City and the London Borough. While it is difficult to explain the higher profile of 14-year-olds than 15-year-olds in both locations from such a relatively small sample, NSPCC project work has continued to engage with a disproportionately higher number of young women aged 14 than aged 15. There is continuing project work taking place to ascertain the reasons for this discrepancy.

Multiple problems experienced by the young women

Table 2.3 shows the numbers of young women from each location against the particular issues that were presented within the case studies. Details relating to most of these issues are discussed further in Chapters 3 to 5.

Table 2.3 Issues identified by the 55 young women

	London Borough (n=30)	Northern City (n=25)	Total (n=55)
History of intermittent truanting	30	25	55
Regular (at least weekly) binge drinking of alcohol	30	25	55
History of going missing or running away from home/or care	28	25	53
History of familial physical abuse	27	20	47
School non-attender (not on school roll)	24	18	42
Sexual health problems	20	20	40
Has a boyfriend who is physically violent	19	20	39
Has been in care or been looked after by the local authority	21	18	39
Has a boyfriend at least four years older than themselves (see Table 2.6)	18	18	36
Self-harms	18	16	34
Regular (at least weekly) heroin use	15	15	30
Has been bullied at school	15	11	26
History of familial sexual abuse	12	13	25
Works for boyfriend (selling sex for money for boyfriend or selling/ swapping for drugs for his use)	9	14	23
Has been raped	12	10	22
Has a police record (3 young women with offence relating to prostitution)	10	12	22
Is homeless	13	9	18
Has attempted suicide	11	7	18
Has been abducted (held against their will for at least two nights)	7	9	16

Has been abducted by a boyfriend	7	8	15
Has been known to have bullied others at school	6	6	12
Has been pregnant	6	3	9
Has worked with police to press charges against abuser	4	3	7
Has had a baby	4	2	6
Has diagnosed learning difficulties	2	1	3
Has diagnosed mental health problems	2	1	3
Has been in prison	1	2	3

Table 2.3 shows that the most common issues shared by the majority of young women were truanting from school or not being on a school roll; regular (at least weekly) binge drinking of alcohol; having a history of going missing or running away from home or care; having experienced familial physical abuse; having had sexual health problems and boyfriends who are physically violent towards them and having been in care or been looked after by the local authority.

Table 2.4 draws on 25 of the 27 issues identified in Table 2.3. The Table excludes:

(a) incidents where the young woman had worked with the police to bring charges against her abuser (as this was seen as productive working with a problem); and

(b) incidents where the young woman had been abducted by her boyfriend (as these cases are subsumed within data on those abducted).

Table 2.4 shows that the young women faced a number of different problems at any one time. Most were dealing with between 10 and 17 issues of concern. These problems were invariably interlinked, meaning that effective service delivery needed to be able to understand and work with multifaceted problems of, for example, current and previous experiences of violence, substance misuse, running away careers and self-harming behaviour.

Table 2.4 Number of problems experienced by young women at the time of the research

Number of problems	Number of young women
4 to 9	10
10 to 13	26
14 to 17	17
18 to 21	2

Before moving into analysis of the young women's own opinions about these problems, data on heroin use and age discrepancies between the young women and boyfriends are explored in more detail.

Heroin use

As noted above, existing research suggests a high correlation between sexual exploitation, prostitution and substance misuse. As seen in Table 2.3, 100 per cent of the young women who took part in the research had serious problems with their binge drinking of alcohol, four young women being repeatedly hospitalised because of alcohol-related injuries. A disproportionately high number of young women also experienced problems with heroin use. Half of the young women from the London Borough (15 of 30) and 15 of 25 of the young women from the Northern City were regular heroin users, all using heroin at least once a week, some with habits that cost between £35 and £75 per day. Table 2.5 shows that young women from both locations experienced problem heroin use and that there was a steady increase in the number of young women dependent upon heroin with age.

Table 2.5 Regular heroin use (at least weekly use) of young women by age

Age	London Borough	Northern City	Total using heroin	Total in age range
13	0	0	0	3
14	2	2	4	13
15	2	1	3	6
16	4	4	8	13
17	5	6	11	14
18	2	2	4	6
Total	15	15	30	55

Violence and relationships with older men

A central theme also identified by previous research as discussed above is the role that a coercive, violent relationship with boyfriends can play in introducing the young woman to sexual exploitation or prostitution.

Thirty-nine of the 55 young women had experienced violent relationships with boyfriends and 47 of the 55 had experienced violence at home from their family or carers. Thirty-six of the 39 young women in violent relationships were with boyfriends who were at least four years older than themselves (see Table 2.6). The violence ranged from being hit, punched, whipped by television wires and phone cables, pushed to the floor and trodden upon (two young women having had their heads stamped upon) through to sexual and emotional intimidation and torture. *L*, aged 17, talked of the pain caused by having had a chilli paste rubbed into her 'private parts', saying that she didn't 'want to remember. It just hurt'. The physical and emotional pain caused by such attacks remained with the young women who needed intensive support by suitably trained workers to begin to speak about and understand the impact that it had had on their lives.

Despite these levels of violence many spoke of emotional attachment to their boyfriends. Only six referred to the boyfriend as a pimp, although 23 of the 39 in violent relationships spoke of selling or swapping sex for money or for drugs for their boyfriend's use. As the focus of the research is on young women's voices, it is their language that is used here. Clearly an outsider's perspective would often redefine the boyfriend as 'pimp' and 'paedophile'.

Table 2.6 clarifies the age discrepancies in more detail, identifying the age ranges of boyfriends of the 36 young women who were in relationships with men at least four years older than themselves. The young women were sometimes reticent about giving their boyfriend's actual age. In these circumstances they were asked to say if the boyfriend was 20 plus, 25 plus, 30 plus, etc. The mean age of boyfriends was calculated by including only those where the age was definitely known.

The Table shows that while all boyfriends were at least four years older than the young women, the majority were in their mid to late twenties. As discussed further in Chapter 6, interventions targeted at supporting young women can be accompanied by efforts to gather evidence to bring cases against abusive men, developing the dual aims of protecting children and prosecuting abusers (Swann and Balding 2002).

Table 2.6 Age of young women and of boyfriends

Age of young woman n=36	Age range of boyfriends	Mean age of boyfriends
14 (n=9)	18 to 28	22
15 (n=8)	20 to 32	25
16 (n=10)	20 to 35	25
17 (n=6)	24 to 51	31
18 (n=3)	26 to 32	28

Categories of risk

Analysis of the nature of the problems when compared against the age range and personal circumstances as illustrated by the young women's language and case studies has suggested three categories of risk.

Category 1: At risk

Running away from home or care, with prolonged periods of truanting from school and going missing. Beginning to engage in emotional and sexual relationships with older, abusive and/or violent men.

Category 2: Swapping sex

Category 1 but with increasing engagement in intense sexual and emotional relationships with older violent men, with increasing misuse of alcohol and drugs, swapping sex for affection, money, drugs, accommodation or other returns 'in kind'.

Category 3: Selling sex

Spending extended periods of time on the street, living in temporary accommodations or being homeless, selling sex and intermittently identifying as working in 'prostitution'.

Young women were placed into one of the three different categories through analysis of their case study material, their own accounts of their lifestyles and activities, and through reference to any existing case file material used for the research with their consent.

The division of the young women into one of the three categories emerged during the course of the research work. This classification was not, however, fully enacted until the final analysis which clearly illustrated distinct stages of vulnerability and exposure to sexual exploitation. The placement of the young women into one of the three categories followed a three-stage process. Firstly, the Choice and Opportunity Project Coordinator drew evidence from the case study data presented, placing each of the young women into one of the three categories. Invariably the decision was made through direct reference to the young women's own narrative, much of which was clearly describing either risk of exploitation, actual swapping of sex for return of favours or selling sex on the street. Secondly, the decision was then checked with the two research officers who had worked with the young women concerned. Finally, the NSPCC manager or other relevant staff who had been involved with the case study material were consulted on the categorisation.

Analysis of the age range of young women within each category of risk shows how movement from category 1 to category 3 takes place with age (see Table 2.7). While young women from different age groups are found in categories 1 and 2, it is evident that older young women (aged 16 and up) are found in category 3, 'Selling sex', all but one self defining as working in prostitution.

Table 2.7 Category 1 to 3 by age

Age	Category 1: At risk n=19	Category 2: Swapping sex n=15	Category 3: Selling sex n=21
13	3	0	0
14	7	6	0
15	3	3	0
16	4	2	7
17	2	3	9
18	0	1	5

The young women's own narratives demonstrate erratic and fluctuating behaviour in their everyday lives, with periods of calm and stability at home followed by episodes of disruption and periods of unrest. The case studies do not all show clear progression from one category of risk to another, and not every young woman moved through the three stages identified. Some, in response to a specific event or series of activities, talked of wanting total independence, running from home and misusing drugs to a later return to a period of stability, never to run again. For example, C, aged 14, began to run away from home for short periods. Demonstrating overtly sexualised behaviour, she talked of seeking out older men to spend time with, when away from home. Following recognition that she had recently been raped, support and intervention helped to provide a framework to prevent the repeated running and offer some stability at home. The running did decrease and C became able to talk more openly to address some of the sexualised behaviour she had been demonstrating. Also, M, aged 16, placed in category 1 'At risk', had been intermittently running away from her home where she lived with her aunt and grandmother since being raped by a family friend when 11 years old. She had become sexually active whilst going missing, with concern expressed about her being abused by older men. After contacting health professionals for treatment for two different sexually transmitted infections and after a short period of accommodation in a children's home, she moved to supported accommodation and experienced a period of stability: speaking of wanting 'to get married, have children and have a proper career'. (It is important to note here that young women were encouraged to provide their own images of their desired futures. With this freedom, the young women invariably appeared to long for a 'normal' existence: seeing 'normal' goals as of getting married and having children.)

The case studies suggested that the young women moved intermittently backwards and forwards between the categories, rather than following a fixed line, a snakes and ladders sequence of movement as opposed to a steady, regular unidirectional progression. This is explored further in Chapters 3 to 5. Many of the problems, identified in Table 2.3, exist for young women in each of the categories of risk. For example, there is little variation between categories 1 to 3 in their histories of previous sexual and physical abuse, experiences of having been 'looked after' by the local authority, of self harming and attempting suicide, or of having been raped or abducted.

However, although young women experienced many of the same sorts of problems, more experienced new problems as they moved from category 1 to 3. For example, although all young women from each of the three categories had histories of intermittent running away from home, those staying away for longer periods, swapping or selling sex, were more vulnerable to risk of other associated problems such as homelessness, regular heroin use and to committing offences.

Table 2.8 illustrates how the number of problems increases as the young women moved from category 1 to 3.

As can be seen from Table 2.8, the numbers of young women in category 3 experiencing these problems was higher than those in category 1. Table 2.9 shows that there was also a steady increase in the number of problems experienced by young women from categories 1 to 3.

Despite this escalation shown in Table 2.9 in the number of problems confronted at any one time, the number of young women who reported contact with social services departments throughout the 18 months within which the research took place was lower for those in category 3 than in category 1. Eighteen of the 19 young women in category 1 had contact with social services, 13 of the 15 in category 2, and 10 of the 21 in category 3. It may be expected that, as most of those in category 1 were younger, they would be more likely to be in touch with social services departments, and that it is the older young women on the street who all services find difficult to engage with. Despite this, the needs presented by young women placed in category 3 were compounded by the problems identified in Table 2.8.

Table 2.8 Numbers of young women experiencing problems by category of risk (Table identifies those problems that escalated across Categories 1 to 3).

	Category 1 At risk of sexual exploitation n=19	Category 2 Swapping sex n=15	Category 3 Selling sex n=21
Has violent boyfriend	11	12	16
Homeless	4	3	15
Regular (weekly) use of heroin	5	6	19
Sexual health problems	15	16	20
School non-attender (not on a school role)	10	12	20
Police record (three of the offences were offences related to prostitution)	3	6	13
Have been in prison	0	0	3

Table 2.9 Escalation of the range of number of problems experienced by young women in categories 1 to 3

	Category 1	Category 2	Category 3
Number of problems experienced by young women	4–15	7–16	4–21*
Average number	9	12	16

* The case study of only one young woman from category 3 identified four problems. The remainder noted more than 11 problems per case.

Racial origin and categories of risk

Existing work suggests that black and ethnic minority young people running from home may be less visible to service providers, many of their associated difficulties going unnoticed (Patel 1994). Table 2.10 notes that all but two of the young women selling sex on the street (those placed in category 3), self defined as white UK, with young women from other self defined racial origins in category 1, At risk, and category 2, Swapping sex. This raises the question of whether it is mainly white young women who progress to sell sex on the street or whether it is that they are more visible, or more easily accessed by project work and research? As noted above, outreach work took place with the specific intention of contacting hard to reach and 'hidden' populations, a range of streets being used for outreach at different times of the day and night. As the

Asian young women in category 2 were involved in intimate, abusive relationships with boyfriends, it may be that subsequent sale of sex (if it took place) was confined indoors, away from the street. Further work is needed to develop the understanding of the relationship between location, race and racism and sexual exploitation.

Table 2.10 Self defined racial origin and category of risk

	Category 1: At risk	Category 2: Swapping sex	Category 3: Selling sex	Total
White UK	12	7	19	38
Black African/ Caribbean	1	2		3
Mixed race white/ Black African/Caribbean	1	1	1	3
Bengali	2			2
Bangladeshi	2	3		5
Somali	1	1		2
Mixed race Maltese/Turkish		1		1
Maltese			1	1
Total	19	15	21	55

Conclusion

This chapter has explained the aims and research methods employed by The Choice and Opportunity Project. It has discussed some of the ethical issues facing the research team and has given an overview of quantitative data drawn from the 55 case studies. It has identified the multiple problems facing young women at risk of, or currently involved with, sexual exploitation or prostitution. The next three chapters focus on the voices of the young women, as recorded in the qualitative data. Chapter 3 focuses on narrative from young women placed in category 1: those at risk of sexual exploitation. Chapter 4 explores some of the issues facing young women who are experiencing prolonged periods of running away from home or care and who are swapping sex for accommodation, money, drugs or other returns in kind. Chapter 5 addresses the issues identified by the young women who are selling sex, self defining as prostitutes.

3. Category 1: At risk of sexual exploitation

'I brushed the fire but didn't get burnt'
(S, aged 17)

Introduction

Young women were placed into Category 1: being at risk of sexual exploitation when there was no clear evidence of them swapping or selling sex, but practitioners, and the young women themselves, noted signs that this had the potential to happen. As seen above, the majority of the 19 young women placed in this category were aged 13 to 15, the oldest being 17. All young women in this category had problems with alcohol abuse, drinking to excess at least once a week. Five of the 19 young women had used heroin at least once a week, four were homeless, three had police records for shoplifting offences, seven had boyfriends over four years older than themselves (all but one aged 20 to 35), 11 had relationships with boyfriends who were violent towards them, four had been abducted by boyfriends, nine had been raped and four had been pregnant. Seventeen of the young women were regularly running away from home or care, ten being off a school roll. Ten of the young women were regularly self harming, seven of whom had made suicide attempts. Fifteen of the young women had experienced sexual health problems.

The chapter is divided into four sections; each identifying early warning signs that a young woman is at risk of sexual exploitation.

Sexualised risk taking and sexual health problems

Adolescence can be a time for risk taking, conflict and rebellion against authority. While young women's desire for rebellion can be exploited by adults to their own advantage, the young women could themselves use the fear and sensation generated by risky sexual relationships with older men as a tool for rebellion. This also has the consequence of drawing attention to the young women's vulnerability to the range of problems she experienced. The riskier her behaviour, the more transparent her vulnerabilities became. It is this complicated relationship between risk taking and vulnerability, that young women may experience in the early stages of running away from home and becoming sexually active, that abusers are sophisticated in identifying and using to their advantage.

For example, *J*, aged 14, generated fear for her welfare in those professionals caring for her, as a mechanism to attract attention to herself. She felt that her own needs and her attachment to her mother had been overlooked when, because of revelations of previous sexual abuse, she was removed from her family home and accommodated by the local authority. She spoke of having been 'picked up' and taken into police protection when suspected of selling sex on the street. Although she refuted claims that she was selling or swapping sex for favours, she explained to the social work staff she was referred on to, that she 'shagged 26 blokes in seven months, I'm not worried about AIDS'. She noted that 'I would return to this if I'm not allowed to go home to live with my mum'. She explained her actions as a means of making the social work staff listen to her. She continued to run from her children's home, often to spend time with her violent older boyfriend with whom she was in love. She did, however, show little awareness of his exploitation of her circumstances. Instead of helping her to identify, and work with, her problems at home and within her care plan, he continued to encourage her to run, by providing a false 'safe haven', increasing her dependency upon him and introducing her to drug misuse and to other older men. While attention seeking and testing behaviour is expected of adolescence, *J* acted out more extreme measures in response to her extreme circumstances. In this case *J* used sexualised risk-taking behaviour as a means of generating attention to her situation. This 'playing with risk' was exploited by an older man she perceived to be a boyfriend. Analysis of the 55 case studies suggested that a number of young women felt isolated from genuine support offered by adults, often turning instead to friendship offered by potential abusers.

Similarly, *B*, aged 14, had been increasingly drawing attention to herself through talking of having sex with older men and being promiscuous. She was recovering from having been abducted by her 21-year-old boyfriend who had locked her in his bedroom for three days and nights. Despite two productive meetings where *B* talked of being sexually active, the researcher's notes recorded that 'she said after two meetings that she didn't want to be involved with the research'. *B* went missing for a few days and was then seen locally 'hanging around' with older men around the taxi rank and park area. Two weeks after *B* had said that she did not want to be involved, the researcher came across her sitting 'with drunks' in the local park. *B* approached the researcher, crying, saying that she was having nightmares and flashbacks about the abduction. From here the working relationship between *B* and the researcher continued. This work with *B* revealed that she returned to sexualised risk-taking behaviour at times when she felt most depressed and despondent. Such activities clearly made her vulnerable to sexual exploitation.

The sexualised risk taking noted above carries vulnerability to risk of infection from sexually transmitted infections. As noted in Table 2.3, a total of 40 of the 55 young women were undergoing treatment for sexual health problems, an additional nine having had unplanned pregnancies. Four of the young women with unplanned pregnancies and 15 of those having undergone treatment for STIs (most commonly syphilis, gonorrhoea and chlamydia) were from category 1: at risk of sexual exploitation. Invariably, the problems arose where young women were unfamiliar with noting or treating STIs; felt unable to exert control over the use of condoms, or, as victims of rape or coercion, were engaging in unwanted sex. The high proportion of young women placed in category 1 with these difficulties suggests that, along with other indicators explored in this chapter, the range of problems with sexual health could be one of the early warning signs of sexual exploitation or coercion.

Conflict at/with school

All 55 young women had histories of truanting from school. Only 13 of the 55 young women were still officially on a school roll, the remaining 42 having decided themselves to leave school through persistent truanting, or having been expelled for non-attendance or disruptive behaviour. However, 35 of the 55 young women were of school age, 17 of whom were in category 1 (at risk), 11 in category 2 (swapping sex for kind) and seven in category 3 (regularly selling sex). Official statistics indicate that the peak age for exclusion from school is 14 years old, most commonly in academic years 10 and 11, the final years of secondary school careers (DfEE 2000 in Osler and others 2002, 23). The 'invisibility' of many of young women's needs within the school environment mean that problems are not noticed or addressed until disruptive behaviour and truancy have escalated to the point where exclusion seems one of the few options available (Osler and others 2002). As 35 of the 55 young women were of school age, contact through educational services such as Education Social Work (Education Welfare Service), off site provision and home tuition provided one of the main resources for identifying young women at risk of, or involved with, sexual exploitation. Despite this, only eight of the 35 had maintained contact with Home Tuition, an Offsite Unit or Pupil Referral Unit offered by the Education Department. This means that 27 of the young women of school age (under 16 years) had no contact with any educational provision.

Although some individual young women noted that they wanted GCSEs, with specific ideas of their own need for career development, their case studies showed continued conflict with school. As poor school attenders, with histories of running away from home, going missing, either being bullied or bullying others, the young women presented a challenge to the school environment. For example, the discussion below with *F*, aged 14, shows that one of the many conflicts she experienced at school pivoted around expectations of age-specific behaviour.

> **Researcher:** What do you think that you should be able to do?
> What do you think is right for a 14-year-old girl to be able to do?
>
> **F:** What she wants. Sleep out when you want. Not go to school when you don't want to. Sleep with anybody you like…
>
> **Researcher:** Do you really?
>
> **F:** No, that's just my life story.

Talking of her wishes for her own future, *F* noted that she wanted children of her own but that she would not want them to have to go through her experiences:

> **Researcher:** …but say you had a daughter and she got to your age, 14. Would you be happy with her sleeping with an older man and stuff?
>
> **F:** Well no, because she'd just be following in my footsteps and I wouldn't want that.

F acknowledged that she aimed to make her own decisions, doing what she wanted as if an adult. She set herself apart from others, noting that her life story was different. She continued to argue that one of the reasons she truanted from school was because she did not want to be treated as a child.

> **Researcher:** …do you feel different at school?
>
> **F:** Yeah, I feel like a kid.
>
> **Researcher:** You feel like a kid. Is that nice?

F: No. I don't want to be like a kid being told what to do and that. Having to do stuff. I like being able to do what I want. Being with adults and them treating me like an adult. When I'm not with them *(adults)* I feel like a kid and I don't like that. (Our italics)

This desire to be treated like an adult was picked up by the school and had been the focus of their follow up work. While it was not possible to maintain regular attendance, *F* was given support through off site provision and by continued outreach from education social work provision. Eventually, through a later period of stability, *F* was able to return to school and continue with her studies. Although behind, she was able to study the syllabus of two GCSEs, an achievement for which she felt proud. This gave an example of the role that the school could play in helping young women identify, and move through, periods of instability.

Similarly *K*, aged 13, described how she had been bullied at school, as a consequence of being open about her sexual relationship with her 14-year-old boyfriend. She felt that this bullying had then led to her acting out: getting into cars with unknown older men and bullying others. She got into trouble with the police for getting into fights and was banned from the local McDonalds. However, she was able to maintain contact with the school and was referred by them to a pupil referral unit.

Many of the early warning signs demonstrated by the young women revolved around either truancy from, or misbehaviour at, school. Twenty-six of the 55 young women noted experiences of being bullied, a further eight saying that they themselves bullied others on a regular basis. The case study material helped to explain some of the contexts for this behaviour. For example,

> *E*, aged 14, was living with foster carers and was on a school roll but was truanting, going missing and spending time in the local park. Her boyfriend, aged 18, was a known local pimp. Experiencing severe problems with alcohol abuse, she had been found unconscious because of excess alcohol and had been hospitalised four times for alcohol-related injuries. Despite being a regular truant, she was still in touch with her local school; bullying and being aggressive when present. Although full of conflict, the contact with school was important to her and she was trying to be receptive to attempts made by the Education Welfare Service to work with her behaviour and support her continued attendance.

A, aged 14, who was abducted by two older men and held against her will for a week, had no previous history of running away. Since the abduction she was an intermittent school attender. Offering her support, the school encouraged her to attend their own support club for young people who had been bullied. Taking up this offer she was able to maintain contact with the school. If she truanted or went missing, she felt able to approach the club on her return. She has subsequently worked with the police to identify her abductors.

L, aged 15, attended a special school for children with learning difficulties. She was noticed to leave in school hours and getting into unknown men's cars. The school raised this with her and in a sex education class she started to talk explicitly about having sex. Follow up work was instigated in an attempt to support her through understanding the dangers of getting into cars, of the nature of abuse and of potentially abusive adults.

Where schools were able to identify and work with these early warning signs, young women could be offered some support to begin to address the issues facing them. The examples above suggest that support groups run within the school, or referral to offsite provision, can provide a context for some young women to maintain contact with educational resources. Despite these examples of good practice it is important to recall that 27 of the young women of school age were not accessing any educational resource, suggesting isolation from one, if not the main, source of social and educational stimuli in transition to adulthood. As discussed more fully in Chapter 6, it is essential to supply outreach support to the young people during the earliest signs of sexual activity within potentially exploitative relationships, irrespective of whether the young person is able to take up the support offered at the time. Schools can play an important role in helping to identify some of these early stages. Chapter 6 notes how specialist staff can work alongside schools to facilitate communication between themselves, alternative educational provision and the young women concerned.

Getting into men's cars

Another 'early warning sign' for risk of sexual exploitation was of young women talking of 'getting into men's cars'. Twenty-two of the 30 young women from the London Borough and 23 of the 25 young women from the Northern City (a total of

45 of the 55 young women) talked of regularly 'getting into men's cars'. While young women who were routinely involved in selling sex spoke of getting into cars with a punter, many of the younger women, and those from categories 1 and 2 (who did not self define as selling sex) were also getting into cars. Nine of the 22 young women from London, and nine of the 23 young women from the Northern City who were regularly getting into men's cars were aged between 13 and 15. In total, 11 of the 19 young women in category 1 (at risk) and 14 of the 15 young women in category 2 (swapping sex) talked of getting into men's cars. These young women were not involved in the routine selling of sex and were getting into cars for reasons other than being picked up by a punter. Their reasons varied: from wanting the thrill of a ride, to escaping from bad feelings or responding to the attention given to them by the older drivers.

The case studies illustrated two categories of 'men in cars': those who appeared to be 'cruising' around, attracted to, or looking for, advances made by a young woman on the street and pulling over to pick her up. In these incidents 'getting into men's cars' meant being picked up for a ride, the consequences of which were unknown but which would not necessarily be violent. A second category of 'men in cars' was those who targeted specific areas where they knew young women might congregate. From the research evidence, these places were local parks, children's residential homes or a specific taxi rank. The men driving these cars appeared to be familiar with the young women, could be connected to a current or past boyfriend and would be more likely to take the young woman to a flat intending to have sex. The examples below, drawn from young women's stories, demonstrate contact with men in cars from both categories.

Immediately after having been sexually abused in the local park by a pupil from her school, *L*, aged 15, started getting into men's cars as a means of temporarily escaping from her local area. She would walk along the street, attract a driver's attention where possible, looking for an opportunity to go for a ride. This activity would mean that she was taken away from her immediate home area for a while and that her thoughts were diverted from the pain of her current situation.

Similarly, *P* talks of getting into cars as an attempt to feel better; to deal with being depressed.

> I get into cars with men I don't know, take drugs and do bad
> things because I am depressed.
> *(P, aged 16)*

M, aged 15, also used 'getting into cars' as a means of temporary escape from being depressed. This was noted by staff of the pupil referral unit she attended, as they identified that getting into cars coincided with increasing incidents of her cutting herself, making extensive use of her phone at school and going missing.

Often, as seen from the examples above, getting into men's cars was identified, and worked with, by school staff or professionals involved in case work. Many times however, getting into men's cars remained unnoticed or not addressed.

For example, *S*, aged 17, was frequently running from home where her father, who had severe mental health problems, and her brother physically abused her. Having been through eight placements in the previous 18 months, she had attempted suicide through overdosing on painkillers and was developing anorexia, becoming increasingly thin and inducing vomiting after eating. *S* stated that she first started getting into cars as a means of generating excitement and providing relief from the pressures she felt under. She started to

> go out with my friend. Getting into boy's cars. That's when we
> used to get the 'beep', 'beep', 'beep', (*car horn*) but I never used
> to know what life was then as well. I used to get into anyone's car,
> but I never had sex with them or nothing like that. I just went for
> cruises or pictures. (Our italics)

S's getting into cars was not identified or worked with at the time. When absconding from care she would disappear between 1 and 2 a.m., being picked up by two men who appeared to target the home. She would be dropped back to the home, sometimes after one or two hours, sometimes longer. The researcher's diary notes that

> after intense support from placement staff (daily meetings with
> residential staff plus three hours per week with the clinical
> psychologist) she seemed to settle down. She was told that she
> could stay until 18 and she was very happy with this. But, after
> confronting a member of staff with a knife, the decision for her
> to stay was reviewed and she was moved on. (Researcher's notes)

Whilst the intense support by placement staff was on offer, her behaviour was slowly being addressed. However, once this support had to be withdrawn, her running away and getting into cars escalated.

That getting into cars for a ride can escalate into swapping sex for a journey is apparent. Drivers, either those cruising or driving for business as taxi or cab drivers, are in a position to exploit young women's desire for excitement, relief and distraction, or simply for a drive from one place to another. For example, *H*, aged 15, had been in foster care after being raped by a member of her extended family and went missing from placements, usually to flats used by dealers and pimps. Talking of returning to the care home when 'starving hungry', she explained that she negotiated a ride in a taxi in exchange for a 'blow job'. *K*, aged 14, talked of having once swapped sex for money when running from care. She was with another young woman who encouraged her, saying that swapping sex for money was an easy way to get cash. *K* said that she found it frightening and would not do it again. However, she continued to go missing and explained that she would flag down cars on the main road outside the residential home asking men if they wanted blow jobs in exchange for cigarettes, alcohol or a ride in the car.

'Getting into cars' is an early indicator of young women's risk of sexual exploitation. It is one of the early risk factors that can be identified and worked with to help raise the young women's awareness to potential danger and abuse.

The phone – a connection to the outside world

The extensive use of the phone was another 'early warning sign' identified by young women and their carers. For example, *K* (13 years) who it was feared was being groomed for sexual exploitation by her mother's boyfriend (a known pimp), talked to the project worker about her own concerns that she was responsible for over £400 worth of the recent home landline telephone bill. Although she did not say that the calls were to boyfriends, she talked of using the phone when at home between periods of running away. She explained use of the phone as an escape route from home and the domestic violence she was witnessing between her mother and her mother's boyfriend.

C, aged 14, had been running from home since the age of 11 when, following her grandmother's death, she moved to live with her mother who was physically violent towards her. Being sexually active but without a regular boyfriend, her crack habit developed, along with the increasing running from home. Her dependency on the phone simultaneously increased as she maintained contact with various dealers, a dependency noted by staff at the education department pupil referral unit, until her home phone was disconnected as a quarterly bill for over £1,000 could not be paid.

The phone can be a resource that enables the young women to communicate with friends and those who offer help. It is however, also a vehicle for manipulation by exploitative adults. Learning to use the phone without creating unmanageable bills is a task for all adolescents, one that is difficult enough for those with regular and consistent support.

Although there can be no direct correlation between heavy phone use and risk of sexual exploitation, a young woman's chaotic, overuse of the phone could possibly be one early warning sign that she may be experiencing increasing problems in negotiating her relationships with friends or boyfriends. Identified at an early stage, support can be offered to help manage the financial difficulties and begin to touch on the underlying manipulation that may be taking place by an exploitative adult using the phone as a means of control.

Conclusion

This chapter has identified some of the early warning signs of sexual exploitation that the young women's case studies have presented. It has noted the important role that schools, pupil referral units, other offsite provision, doctors and sexual health clinics can have in helping to identify and work with these early signs. It has illustrated that young women are facing a range of problems at any one time, needing coordinated responses from a range of service providers. The next chapter addresses some of the issues facing young women who are beginning to swap sex for favours in kind.

4. Category 2: Swapping sex for accommodation, money, drugs or other favours 'in kind'

Introduction

This chapter explores some of the accounts given by the 15 young women placed in the second category: 'Swapping sex'. A significant feature of this group is that the majority had older boyfriends, all of them violent. Eleven of the 15 young women had boyfriends aged 18 and over. Seven of these 11 were aged 16 and under (four aged 14, two aged 15 and one aged 16). Seven of the young women in category 2 had been abducted and held against their will.

Of the 15 young women, all had serious alcohol problems, two having been hospitalised for alcohol-related injuries. All had a history of truanting from school and all had experienced physical abuse from carers.

Table 4.1 Profile of the 15 young women placed in category 2

15	experienced problems with sexual health
14	talked of getting into men's cars for a ride or for a specified journey
12	were school non-attenders
12	had a history of self harming
7	had been abducted
6	regular heroin users (compared to five in category 1 and 19 in category 3)
6	held police records
5	had been raped
5	had worked closely with the police to press charges against their abductor
4	had made suicide attempts
2	were technically homeless
2	had diagnosed mental health problems

The following two sections cover the main issues raised by these young women in their case study work. It is important that while these issues are described under separate headings, the interrelationship between them is not lost. The young women were invariably traumatised and deeply affected by familial abuse, which had often been transferred from generation to generation. While specific issues are separated in the discussion below, when considering the total predicament faced by these young women, they should not be seen in isolation.

Running away

A risk factor established here, and in previous research/project work, is the connection between running away from home or care and vulnerability to sexual exploitation. Eighty-nine per cent of the young women in category 1 and 100 per cent of young women in both categories 2 and 3 identified histories of running away from home or care. As will be seen later, it is invariably through running that the young women become increasingly vulnerable to poverty, hunger, drug and alcohol abuse: all of which place them at risk of exploitation. Running away has been noted as a sign of young people's own confusion and distress (Home Office 2001). This is confirmed in the young women's stories.

Making a new start

Many young women talk of running, not only to get away from circumstances that they found impossible to tolerate, but also as a means of trying to make a fresh start. Running was an attempt to make a positive move away from a negative history. This is explained in reference to case study material. It was through the process of running that the young women attempted to gain some control over their circumstances. However, while the young woman may have been making an attempt to be assertive, she was simultaneously increasing her vulnerability to manipulation by abusers (Ivison 1998).

For example, A, aged 14, who lived with both parents, was abducted by her boyfriend when running away from home. Talking of why she ran, A explained that she wanted to escape from her mother who was concerned about A's relationship with her older boyfriend

> she just wouldn't have it so I ran away. I weren't going with him
> at first and she was giving me grief so I ran away.

Wanting her independence, she ran away from home, going to her 'boyfriend' who then abducted her and held her against her will, raping her and starting a long string of violent encounters with him. Similarly, *K*, aged 15, noted that she ran to escape the confusion that she felt about her behaviour when at home:

> I used to come back home. I used to go out 24/7 to get things out of my head, when I was at home I didn't know what I was doing.

S, aged 16, was intermittently swapping sex for drugs and money. She had been diagnosed as clinically depressed with post traumatic stress disorder. She suffered from suicidal thoughts, had attempted to kill herself through an overdose, stabbed and cut herself and spoke of 'taking pills' (taking three or four paracetamol two or three times a day when distressed). She stopped going to school when 13 years old because of 'family problems'. Her father was frequently hospitalised, with physical health problems, her older brother with whom she lived was physically violent towards her and she was abducted and raped by members of her extended family when 13. Suffering from repeated sexual health problems, *S* got into cars with men she didn't know and went missing for two to three days at a time when events at home were too much for her to feel able to handle.

By contrast, *P*, aged 16, ran in order to avoid the professionals who were trying to help her, because she felt she could not face discussing her problems. Rather than work with professionals to identify the problems, she wanted to run, to move away from them. She noted that

> after four months I started drinking. They first put me into foster parents. They thought I needed my head…they thought there was something going on at home I wasn't telling them and so I got pissed off; and that was the first time I ran away from home. I thought people are messing up my life, I've to hide from them.
> *(P, aged 16)*

On return, the care home and project staff were consistent with their message that they wanted to offer support. With time, *P* reached a position where she felt able to talk about her past problems and engage with project work to begin to look forward constructively.

N, aged 14, also ran because she could not stay within her situation without doing something: 'I cannot bear to do nothing'. The researchers' field notes explained that *N* talked of being taken over by gloomy thoughts when at home and that she was fearful that her life would engulf her. *N* ran to move away from these feelings.

Similarly, *J*, aged 17, spoke of intermittently running away during the previous two years in attempts to make new starts, to move away from the hardships she had experienced. Explaining her feeling about being at home with her elder sister, her carer who had abused her physically and sexually, *J* said:

> (I) used to stay in my bedroom for two months, I couldn't get out. I even tried to commit suicide as well…I tried to take some tablets. I just didn't see point in living no more and because of what my sister was doing to me it kind of like, topped it all, and made it worse…
>
> **(J, aged 17)**

After reaching a point when she did eventually decide to run, she was raped on the street. This led her to services for support. However, once placed in a children's home she continued to run, not in her eyes as a negative step but as a means of coping with her confusion:

> just going out and just putting it behind me and raving…I stayed out one night, coming in the next day and also they thought that J is not handling it, since she got raped and she is not handling the situation very well, but people find different ways to handle things…some people might like going for walks to clear their heads and some people might like to not even talk about it, put it behind them and just move on…

Although *J* spoke of wanting her own privacy and space to sort herself out, she did still receive intensive support from the staff each time she returned home. With this help she moved to a position where she could work with her confusing and upsetting past. She disclosed the violence and abuse she had received from her sister when she had lived at home to the police, and felt able to begin to move on with her development, running less frequently from care.

Without condoning running behaviour, it is evident that the young women see running as an opportunity to 'do something', a chance to make a move, to be active and exert some self-determination over what often appear to be impossible situations. The point at which the young woman decided to run and the point at which she decided to return are turning points. Both times the young woman herself was making a decision, trying to gain some control over her life. If suitable support can be maintained at these turning points, the young woman can be encouraged to use her desire for self-determination to her own advantage. As developed in Chapter 6, interventions supporting young women who run need to embrace the young person's attempt to be 'doing something'.

Managing risk

As discussed above, running away from home puts young people at risk of sexual exploitation. This was clearly explained by *Il*, aged 17. She ran from home when she was unable to negotiate the childcare of her baby with her mother. She explained that running was a sign of her vigorous assertion of her own independence, once she realised that her mother was not in a position to share care of her son:

> that's one of the things that made me run away when my son was ten days old. I can't hold him, fine, then you just have him and I'll go about my business. I was on the street for four or five days just eating, Oh God, I can't talk about this... This is just ugh. I used to eat food out of the garbage.

Il used running as a statement to assert how she was going to try to move on, to go about her business. She continued to explain how the desire to run soon changed to a necessity to survive. This meant creating strategies for managing her vulnerability and the risky situations she found herself in. She describes some of the stages that she moved through to find accommodation while on the run.

> I ran away for three months, when I couldn't take it no more out there. I had no food, no nothing. One thing I believed is, don't ever tell...I got tempted to do prostitution. I've slept in men's houses that I don't know and though every day I ran away. But God gave me some intelligence, really I could clap myself for that because I've, most girls that turned to prostitution, but I used to go out there, I'd sit in a pub, act like, you know I just came from work or something, well...I don't have nowhere to go that night...but the thing that I really, is lying. Lying, that got me off...

Il then explained how she would sit in a pub and wait for a man to approach her. She would accept a drink and then, lying, explain that her friend with whom she was going to stay had disappeared. She explained the story of how she dealt with men when in this situation. A short extract of the dialogue recorded shows how she secured a bed for the night. Talking of the hypothetical phone call she had made to her imaginary friend she continued the lie to the man:

> **Me:** She's sick, she's not coming. She's got my money. She's got my house keys. I don't know where to go tonight. She is so stupid, why is she doing this to me?
> **Man:** Don't worry. You can stay at my place tonight and I will take you down to your place tomorrow.

Il continued to explain that she would stay the night with the man and would then repeat the same pattern the next night with a different man until she felt unable to sustain the lifestyle any longer. She also described how she would avoid having to exchange sex for the bed for the night:

> If he tried to do anything I would go, 'Oh, I'm on my period'.
> Why don't you wait until tomorrow, and when tomorrow comes
> I move on. The next man that comes, I do the same thing.
> Sleep at this place, eat, next morning come out. One day I stole
> money from one of them. I wouldn't lie. I stole £123 and
> bought myself some clothes and I couldn't go back to the same
> place because that man that I took the money from, that's his
> regular place so I just decided OK, this is just about it, go
> home. You can't take no more.

K, aged 16, also talks of using a man's flat, being given a key and staying there in exchange for sex when running from her residential placement. She was desperate for a place to stay and spoke of the man as her boyfriend to whom she turned during periods of stress. After having encouraged her to use the flat, he locked her in, raped her and tried to force her into having sex with his friends.

R, aged 14, was found in two men's flat by the police after having gone missing. She spoke of having been offered accommodation, which she needed as she felt unable to return home. She was then held there against her wishes, and raped by one of the two men before he released her to return home.

A, aged 14, also ran from home and stayed overnight with men that she did not know. She exchanged sex for a bed for the night, talking of sleeping with a man in his early 30's because he let her stay with him. For this brief time, she considered the man to be her boyfriend. She explained that while she was there she was asked to sleep with other men, being encouraged to bring other 'girls' into the flat. There were about 12 men aged 20 and over, with about six young women aged between 14 and 15 intermittently attending the flat. She talked of one young woman who came and felt unsafe. This young woman shocked *A* by saying that *A*'s boyfriend was a sex dealer. It was at this point that *A* decided to move on, returning to the street and then home. With later follow up work *A* was able to report the 'boyfriend' to the police. This provided a useful illustration of effective inter-agency work: in this case between voluntary agency project staff, statutory social services departments and the police. The voluntary organisation drop in provision was used by the young woman, who then gained confidence to inform statutory services of her abuse. It also demonstrates the importance of peer pressure, *A* feeling shocked into seeing the truth about her boyfriend because of the comments of a peer.

H, aged 15, showed how such communication between young women on the run can be important, but fraught with tension in difficult circumstances. Talking at the end of the research project about the impact of having been involved, *H* notes that:

> I'm on a health and beauty course at college now. I didn't see
> myself as vulnerable to being used sexually but to drug use,
> because of the area where I live, loads of kids use smack...I went
> out with J (her boyfriend) to get at this girl that I didn't like.
> I knew what I was doing, but now I feel used by him...You should
> talk to C (a friend). She's vulnerable, very. She's stupid, she
> sleeps with the lads for fags and drink, you know. That's why I
> lost it with her the other night and now I'm being done for GBH.

The research and project staff discussed the possibility that *H* took her frustration out on *C* for being 'stupid' instead of being able to vent her anger towards the 'lads'. Such displaced and random displays of young women's anger were prevalent throughout the research work. The 'lads' were a group of men who were known locally to be violent and who regularly brought young women into their flat. They were later the focus of a successful joint police and social services investigation into the sexual exploitation of young people in the local area.

Abduction and rape

As shown in Table 4.2, a total of 16 young women had been abducted, with 15 of these abductions undertaken by men the young women referred to as their boyfriends. Abduction was defined by the research team as when the young woman spoke of being held against her will; their own language described 'not being able to get out', or 'locked in'. The length of time that young women spoke of being held varied from one day to a week.

Table 4.2 Abduction and rape

	Young women abducted	Abducted by 'boyfriends'	Raped
Category 1	4	4	9
Category 2	7	6	5
Category 3	5	5	8
Total	16	15	22

Three of the 16 young women had been abducted by the same man, each calling him her boyfriend. These three young women worked later with the social services department and the police to report and press charges against their abuser. Three other young women were abducted by their regular boyfriends, six were abducted by men (they referred to as their boyfriends) who provided them with accommodation whilst they were running from home and one was abducted by a man she called her boyfriend and her pimp. Of the remaining three young women, one was abducted by a punter (who she called her boyfriend) who had picked her up from the street, and two were held against their will by members of their extended family, one referring to the abuser as her boyfriend at the time. Some of the young women were scared of further violence if they were to report their abductors or 'boyfriends' to the police. Others were concerned that they would not be believed and felt frightened of further questioning if they were to report. For example, P, aged 15, argued that she was reluctant to pursue charges against her uncle who, with support of other relatives, abducted and raped her. She felt that no professional would believe what had happened to her, deciding instead to run from home after the abduction.

> They think 'Oh she's making up stories', because I didn't have
> enough evidence and I was drugged at the time. My relatives
> drugged me. My uncle worried that as I was under 16, the police
> would find me…

Those who had been abducted whilst running away were afraid that they would get into trouble if they disclosed where they had been whilst on the run. Despite this, seven of the 16 young women had reported incidents of abduction to the police and social services departments, leading to action being brought against three men.

Returning to the experiences of those who run away from home, it can be seen that young people are particularly vulnerable to violence, abuse and abduction when isolated on the streets. That the activities described by the young women when they were on the run were dangerous is evident both to them and to those responsible for their care. It is similarly worrying that, as noted by P above, the impact of trauma often remains unspoken. The young women were, however, experimenting with ways of trying to be in control of the dangers in their lives, fluctuating between tension at home and violence and danger on the street. This calls specifically for continued and relentless attempts to intervene in the early stages of a running career. Supported outreach, street based work and coordinated inter-agency provision needs to target young people following abduction and exploitation. This needs to be premised on the understanding that many will be wavering in their attempts to make brave, self-determined steps away from intolerable situations, while being unaware of all the dangers they may face.

Young people in abusive relationships

As explored in Chapter 1, previous research and project work with young women experiencing sexual exploitation has argued that the existing child protection discourse is not applicable on its own as an approach to underpin practice interventions. While there remains the commitment to protect the child from abuse from exploitative adults, the child protection frameworks do not fully address the complex and complicated ways that the young people are involved in emotional and sexual relationships with adults. Neither can they, on their own, respond to the complicated sexual health issues arising for the young women (Noell and others 2001). While it is not disputed that sexually abused children also have complicated emotional ties with their abusers, the child protection framework, policy and practice does not fully connect with the range of complexities associated with adolescence, sexual activity and sexual exploitation. These can include the interrelationship between drug misuse and alcohol dependency, sexual health issues, the need for accommodation and money, the search for independence and the escape from abuse through relationships with older, exploitative, invariably violent, men who pose as boyfriends.

Instead, the stories presented by many of the young women are similar to those revealed by descriptions of emotional and physical abuse through domestic violence. For example, *N*, aged 16, described as an A star GCSE pupil by her school, where she maintained intermittent attendance, lived at home with her aunt, had a history of running from home to avoid physical violence, had been diagnosed as clinically depressed and had a history of self harming. She discussed the reasons that she did not leave her boyfriend, *K*, a heroin addict aged somewhere between 25 and 35. She did not leave, despite the fact that he has increasingly introduced her to 'street life', abducted her for a week and raped her, kicked her, tried to strangle her and created a fear that he could kill her. Although she wanted to return to study, she explained that she could not because she 'loves him'. In an unsent letter to him she says:

> I never loved anyone the way I loved you, but no one ever hurted
> me the way you have, to make me hate you in the way I do now,
> could never hate anyone the way I hate you, will never love
> anyone the way I loved you

She explained the complicated tangle between love and hate as an obsession, 'he takes up all my head space'. Although she wanted to maintain her school work, the researcher's notes recorded her argument that she was going back to him because:

- if she left him before the police did anything her family may suffer;
- she has had a miscarriage with his baby and she wanted to tell him so he knew how much she has suffered;
- she thought that if she stayed with him for long enough she could change him, make him treat her differently;
- he was dependent upon her, needing her for money for his drugs, he has asked her for £50 and she gave it to him because she has no one else to give it to;
- when he forced her to have unprotected sex it was only because it was his birthday.

The complex emotional demands and responses articulated in the above summary from the researcher's notes are more akin to those expressed by adults in situations of domestic violence than those expressed by children in situations calling for child protection procedures. It is essential, however, that the status of the child, with the associated need for protection from abusive adults, does not become lost. This line of argument is developed in Chapter 6.

Previous and current experiences of violence

Many of the young women came from violent family environments or from families deemed unable to provide appropriate care. Twenty-six reported having been bullied, 47 had experienced physical violence at home (violence either defined as causing 'significant harm' under the Children Act 1989 or self reported by the young women as causing physical injury such as bruising, fracture and/or bleeding). Twenty-five reported histories of sexual abuse. Thirty-nine of the 55 young women were, or had experiences of being, in care, while 41 had received some social work intervention. While caution needs to be applied in assuming deterministic patterns of intergenerational behaviour, many of the young women's narratives show how unresolved feelings of both love and hate towards parents or carers could be carried over into their relationships with older boyfriends.

For example, S, aged 16, a young woman placed in category 2, lived at home with her parents with whom she had a difficult relationship. She had been repeatedly attacked by her violent brother and sexually assaulted by her uncle. She stopped going to school when 13, regularly self abused through cutting, had had three abortions, ongoing treatment for STIs and got into cars with 'men I don't know'. She said that she was in love with her boyfriend, a man over 20 years old, although she knew he was abusive, but 'I cannot let go'. She explains:

> I know he did all that to me, he was just taking it out on me
> because I was only 16 and he thought I didn't know lots of things
> about the world but I did. What he did to me really hurt me, but
> in a way I don't, but in a way I do forgive him because I love this
> boy deep down in my heart.

The boyfriend, clearly able to exploit the unresolved and fraught contradictions that S has felt in her familial relationships, continued her understanding of interpersonal relationships as abusive. He expected her to accept that violence against a child, who, as S says, does not 'know lots of things about the world', is acceptable.

A, aged 14, ran from violence at home and was subsequently accommodated by social services. She had a violent boyfriend. Her confusion between violence and care was demonstrated by her comment that her boyfriend hurt her to 'show that he cares'. He had abducted her and forced her to have sex, although she was reluctant to define it as rape. She felt that her life was out of control, trying to assert herself on the one hand: 'I am not a toy', while being increasingly under her boyfriend's influence to the point of persuading residents from the children's home to scratch (tattoo) his name on her arm.

Similarly, L, aged 17, lived with her mother who was physically violent. She talked of her mother using wire and sticks as instruments for beating her. Talking of her feelings towards her mother, L says:

> Sometimes I wish she was dead and then I wouldn't be worrying
> and I think that it is really horrible to wish someone dead but it's
> how I feel. But she's my Mum. I love her. I thank her for bringing
> me to this world but still I hate it in a way. It's funny you know
> that it is really confusing when you really hate somebody and you
> care for them. That is really bad.

L repeatedly entered violent and abusive relationships with older men who were sophisticated at exploiting her previous experiences of abusive relationships, continuing to confuse the boundaries between love and hate. Through project work contact, she had been able to start to talk about her relationships and her experiences of abuse from boyfriends with whom she disappeared for three to four days at a time. She spoke of feeling numb to the pain, a numbness that helps her to survive.

> I'm just like the one stuck in the middle, like a punch-bag to
> punch left, right and centre whenever you feel like it. Like I
> have no feelings. I don't feel the pain. I don't get hurt. Nothing.

> That I'm just like a human but I don't feel nothing at all. Like
> none of my feelings or my pain or my hurt don't really matter
> much to you because I'm nothing as far as you're concerned.
> *(L, aged 17)*

L had been fearful that receiving support and discussing her experiences of abuse
might interrupt this tactic for coping. Despite this, she was beginning to explore why
it was that she found it 'easier to make friends with men – most of my friends are
male'. She was looking at her severe problems with alcohol abuse, recognised by
project workers but hitherto denied by herself. She had received support in
attending a sexual health clinic and entered an employment scheme. As the levels of
abuse she experienced were high, so too the practice response needed to be
consistent and intense. Through maintaining daily contact with her, project staff
were able to engage her in weekly drop in sessions.

Often however, the support offered was rejected because previous experiences of
care have been confused with abuse. One of the researcher's diary notes captures
this resistance. Talking of efforts to continue work with *M*, aged 15, the researcher
notes:

> she instinctively bats away the warmth and affection she craves –
> as if bound to the notion that if she accepts, it will inevitably be
> withdrawn

and of *S*, aged 17:

> there is a deep-rooted fear of trusting others which places
> relationships in jeopardy... The rejection acts as a device to
> achieve and maintain manageable level of intimacy.

Conclusion

This chapter has focused on the specific issues raised by young women who were
placed in category 2: Swapping sex for return 'in kind'. It notes the young women's
attempts to take some control over their lives, decisions of running from or
returning to home representing turning points where they have decided to 'do
something'. It also notes the ways that young women talk of surviving on the street,
negotiating risk in the search for food and accommodation. The young women's
stories clarify the extent of emotional commitment many feel towards boyfriends
who abuse them and suggest that domestic violence discourses (that appreciate the
impact of practical and emotional dependency within violent interpersonal

relationships) may be helpful when trying to address the problems these young women face. Central to this is an appreciation that victims of violence may take substantial periods of time before being able to think about leaving the perpetrator or recovering from the abuse. The next chapter examines the issues raised in the case studies of young women who were also often in abusive relationships with men and were self defining as prostitutes.

5. Category 3: Selling sex

Introduction

> I don't want to be a junkie. Some crusty girl. I should be living a
> very good life. The way I used to dream when I was a little girl.
> This is not my dream. This is not my dream at all. It's my
> nightmare. The worst nightmare.
> *(I, aged 17)*

> We talked about the eclipse the previous evening. S said that in
> London, where she was, the light resembled the 'orange colour'
> of memories, like the colour of old photographs. She became
> quite excited as she tried to explain what she meant, though
> afraid at the same time that maybe I wouldn't understand. But I
> did and told her so and we felt connected for a moment.
> *(Researcher's field notes from interview with S, aged 16, on the street)*

The two quotations above illustrate the 'nightmare' that many of the young women
experience, and also the importance (and difficulty) of communicating with those
who may help them. This isolation from support runs through the analysis of the
material presented by the young women in this category who experience severe
problems with drug and alcohol abuse and are often in established, abusive
relationships with adults.

This chapter explores some of the ways that young women who are selling sex
explain their circumstances. Twenty-one young women, all aged 16 to 18 inclusive,
were placed in category 3: Selling sex. Twenty of the 21 defined themselves as
prostitutes, the other saying that although she sold sex, she only sometimes saw
herself as a prostitute. Nineteen of the 21 young women were regular heroin users,
the extent of use explored further below. Fifteen of the young women were
homeless, either sleeping rough on the street, with friends or boyfriends, in bed and

breakfast or temporary hostel accommodation. Eighteen had boyfriends who were at least four years older than themselves, 16 of whom were violent. Five of the young women had been abducted by their boyfriends, eight had been raped, 20 had experienced some sexual health problems during the eighteen-month period of the research, and three had had a baby, one maintaining care of her child with her own mother's support. Twelve of the 21 had self harmed, seven having attempted suicide. One of the 21 young women was maintaining attendance at a local college, the remaining 20 were not in touch with any educational provision. Thirteen of the young women had police records, three of whom had been in prison. As noted in Chapter 2, the young women faced a range of different problems, invariably while isolated from support services.

This chapter looks firstly at the reasons given by the young women for starting to sell sex, exploring the relationship between self-esteem, experiences of abuse and selling sex. It then looks specifically at the interplay between drug use and selling sex as described by some of the young women concerned. It identifies the snakes and ladders effect of the movement in and out of selling sex, and then draws on some of the young women's comments of which services they have found to be helpful.

Multiple reasons for starting to sell sex

> I could only get money otherwise by robbing people.
> *(J, aged 16)*

> It's only possible to protect yourself if you think you're worth protecting.
> *(R, aged 17)*

As discussed in Chapter 1, a common question asked of young people who are routinely selling sex is: which came first, the drug use or the selling of sex? Previous work has shown that young people can use drugs to numb the emotional and physical pain of the work but that they also need the money from the work to pay for the drugs (Barrett 1997, Cusick 1998). This does not position either one before the other, but sees them as interdependent. The case studies suggest that it is rarely possible to isolate any one specific reason for starting to sell. Referring to Chapters 3 and 4, it is clear that the young women face a range of problems that make them vulnerable to exploitation and to prostitution. However, when asked when and why they started to sell, a number of reasons were given (see Table 5.1).

Table 5.1 Reasons given by young women for starting and continuing to sell sex

	Starting n=21	Continuing n=21
For drugs	9	11
Coerced by boyfriend (drugs involved in each case)	6	7
To care for own children	1	1
Result of trauma: rape/abortion	3	
Accommodation	1	
Money	1	2

Table 5.2 Age at which the 21 young women started to sell sex

Age	Number of young women n=21
7	1 (see text)
13	2
14	2
15	4
16	3
17	3
Didn't say	6

Six of the young women met on the street did not want to give an age at which they started working. The young woman who had said that she started at the age of seven noted that this was when she first remembered running from home and spending time on the street. She wanted seven put as the age she started because she made a direct association between being on the street and selling sex.

Although boyfriends were given by only six young women as the reasons for starting and by seven as the reasons for continuing, 16 of the young women were in violent relationships with boyfriends for whom they provided money or drugs.

The eight young women who were not in a regular relationship with a boyfriend when they started selling, spoke of beginning for a variety of reasons. One explained that she had needed money for accommodation. Two wanted money for their own drug use; one needed money to pay for bringing up her child and one started because she had been in debt and needed money. She was the only young woman not using heroin and explained that she had been shoplifting to get clothes and the provisions she needed, but that she was 'crap' at that, having been arrested for theft. Three young women started as a direct result of traumatic events, two as a result of being raped, and one because she felt bad about herself for having had her third termination. In this latter case, *K* (aged 17) saw herself as a 'bad person deserving of ill treatment'. Having a heroin and crack cocaine problem, *K* spoke of entering the work because of a lowering of self-esteem related to having had her third termination. Researchers' notes of contact with her on three different occasions over a three-month period gave an insight into this. The diary recorded:

> 14 August: K phoned project. She thinks she is pregnant. I go with her to the clinic, she is pregnant. She says, this is the third time, how could I?

After the termination,

> 25 September: She phones the project. Is distressed. She is finding it difficult to speak. Regrets lots of things. Is upset about her 'baby'. Her boyfriend was violent last night. She wants to kill herself. Says she might drop in.

> She does not drop in. Does not return calls. Has gone missing.

> 29 November: Met K on outreach. She has a new 33-year-old boyfriend. He is homeless, she is working and is down to her last condom. Takes some condoms and says she will keep in touch.

K appeared not to have started working until she began to feel like a 'bad person', which was a consequence of her third termination. It is also significant that she spoke of having a new boyfriend, as this coincided with her starting to sell on the street for the first time. Although drugs were a part of her life, her own accounts and the case study work suggested that she started selling for a number of complicated reasons, finally prompted by feelings of self-hatred and desire for self harm.

The connection between feeling bad about self, self harming and use of the street is likewise evident in the following case examples.

T, aged 16, had a pattern of self-destructive behaviour. She cut her arms saying 'Usually when I'm crying or when I'm sad I like to cut myself'. She went on to explain that when depressed, she spent more time on the street. She wanted semi-independent living, not foster or residential care that her social worker advised for her. Her boyfriend was aged 20, although she had other relationships with older guys, 'dodgy guys', who had bought her clothes. One such 'boyfriend' gave her a mobile phone. He gave her phone 'top-up' cards in return for sex as payment. She managed this situation for a while until ceasing contact with him after he was particularly violent, beating her head. She said that she engaged mostly in clipping, rather than regularly selling sex on the street. However, she spoke of having sex with older men and had been treated for chlamydia and gonorrhoea. For *T*, the self harming through cutting, the use of the street and her sexual activity are spoken about together, all being activities that happened when she felt worse about herself, running from care and 'taking risks'.

Similarly, *E*, aged 16, who has been under a full Care Order, is one of five children, three of whom had been taken into care. While wanting to care for her children, *E*'s mother had struggled with her own problem use of Class A drugs, intermittently selling sex for money for drugs. *E* had long-term problems with binge use of alcohol and went missing from care, returning with money. She had regularly self-harmed, having cut herself on the arms and legs. She spoke of using the street as a place to sell sex and equated this with self-harming, having scratched 'slag' on her own arm.

Issues of self worth and self-esteem also came to the fore in the young women's involvement in abusive relationships. For example, *R*, aged 17, (quoted earlier in this chapter), noted that she would only protect herself from her abusive relationship with her boyfriend if she thought she was worth it. Her case study showed that she started to sell sex and use drugs as a result of coercion from an abusive boyfriend. The model, explained in Chapter 1, where the abuser takes the young woman through different stages of grooming, is helpful here as it illustrates the complex reasons that she is selling sex on the street. As noted, however, the case studies introduced a range of reasons for entering the work alongside relationships with men. These connect to the young women's own personal histories of depression, self abuse, experience of familial violence and activities related to running away (getting into cars, swapping sex for accommodation, being abducted) as discussed in Chapters 3 and 4.

Drug misuse: never an isolated issue

The case studies of the nine young women from Table 5.1, who said that they started working to pay for drugs for themselves, give an insight into the complex interrelationship between their drug use and other problems they experience. While they themselves say that they are working to pay for drugs, the case studies suggest that their circumstances are more complicated than any one clear-cut explanation can offer.

For example, *V*, aged 16, had been selling sex for money to pay for drugs when running from residential care, where she had lived since she was 12. She started using drugs when running from care and has had a heroin problem since the age of 13. She spoke of injecting into both her hands and feet. Her repeated drug misuse has created a number of physical health problems including regular stomach upsets, pelvic inflammatory disease and enuresis.

Although she has worked intermittently for different pimps, she has had the same boyfriend, who is in his 30's, for the last three years. He is controlling, violent and abusive. She has had his child, who was put up for adoption and has had a second pregnancy by him. In the periods of being sober, *V* is energetic and keen to continue her education, although very cautious about talking of her past. Being an avid reader of Harry Potter, when asked of her wishes for the future, she explained that she wanted live on her own and be a criminal psychologist. She explained that she sold sex to pay for the drugs she used and that if she could rid herself of the habit, she would not need to sell. She explained that she could only get the equivalent amount of money by robbing people, but that she was no good at that 'if I had the choice, wouldn't be out here'. She argued that if she did not have a drug problem, everything else in her life would correct itself and she would be happy.

Despite this clarity, she continued to engage in relationships with older men who were emotionally, physically and sexually abusive. She had a low opinion of herself, saying that she 'looks in the mirror and feels disgusting. I feel abused.' She expressed extreme anger towards her mother, an alcoholic, and her father who was dying from cancer-related illnesses. Her brother was violent towards her and was also a heroin addict, encouraging her to make money for the family. That her problems with drug use were related to other issues in her life was apparent, although it was a connection that she herself was reticent to make at this stage. To be able to offer her support in dealing with her addiction would have been a start, but interventions need to maintain a perspective that can accommodate the complex interrelationship between drug misuse, self-esteem, violence and abuse alongside practical considerations such as housing, financial management and physical and sexual health. As the problems presented by the young women are multifaceted, so too do the services offered need to be able to incorporate a variety of therapeutic and practical responses.

Similarly, *K*, aged 17 when first met on outreach, talked of the impact that her previous experiences of abuse had had on her behaviour through her adolescence. During the course of the research she had become increasingly articulate about the many problems that she faced. She had been known to the local Social Services Department since her early teens, having revealed that she had been raped by a family member when she was a child. She explained that she had started swapping sex for accommodation when she was 14, saying that she did not realise at that stage exactly what she was doing. She had two significant boyfriends, both heroin users, who introduced her to drugs and encouraged her to sell sex for money. During periods of running from home she had been abducted, raped and physically attacked. She had convictions for mugging and credit card robbery and spoke of setting punters up to be robbed by pimps. At the point of the first interview she was working for her 51-year-old boyfriend, saying that she wanted to save money to buy a jeep and that, in the future, she hoped to go to college.

Contact was maintained with *K* through outreach until, just after turning 18, she received a prison sentence for soliciting and for theft. When visited in prison by the researcher she spoke more about the feelings generated by the rape by a family member and about the impact that this had had on her behaviour. She had begun to realise her contradictory desires – to run away, using heroin and crack cocaine to block memories, as opposed to attending college and continuing her education. While the young woman had initially explained that she started to sell sex for money for drugs, she became increasingly articulate through the course of the research about the number of complex reasons for starting to sell. These included her response to her previous experiences of abuse and her resulting low self-esteem.

These examples from the case studies illustrate that the young women's use of drugs are a part of a range of problems that they experience. The following section continues to focus on the fluctuation in the use of drugs and selling of sex amongst many of the young women's stories presented in the case studies.

Irregular patterns of selling: the snakes and ladders effect

As is argued in Chapters 3 and 4, it is important not to see the young women's behaviour as static and fixed. While some young women may use the street on a regular basis to sell sex, some may intermittently sell, while others may use the street on a one-off occasion.

For example, *S*, aged 17, had been using heroin on and off since she was 12. She described herself as a binge user. Her regular habit cost her over £100 per week with her average use of 100 grams over four days. She considered this to be a small amount, saying that when bingeing her costs went up dramatically and her need to work increased. She binged when 'hassled' by dealers and boyfriends. Preferring to be left alone to get on with her life, she became nervous and anxious when with others and binged as a means to try to 'forget or disappear'. She maintained intermittent attendance at the NSPCC project drop in. On one occasion dealers were harassing her over the phone, offering her £3,000 if she would work with them. She knew that she would not be given that amount of money but was nervous that they were phoning and wanted to be able to 'disappear'. However, at the same time, the dealers supplied her with heroin for her own use and so she felt trapped in relying on those she wanted to avoid. She noted that during periods when she felt happier she was more in control of her use of heroin, used the street less as a place to run to, and reduced the amount of time spent selling sex. She was happier when her boyfriend, aged 28, also a heroin user, was nice to her and when she felt that there was some hope for her future. However, she explained that when her boyfriend was violent, her use of heroin, and need to sell sex for money, escalated.

B, aged 17, had been regularly selling sex and using heroin for three years. Her use of the street as a place to sell reduced since she met a new boyfriend, originally a punter, who seemed to genuinely care for her and was supporting her into drug rehabilitation. She spoke of the frequency with which she worked diminishing since she had been with this boyfriend. Contact with *B* had been gained through outreach work. The researcher's notes record that during an outreach session, *B* yelled for them to come over to her, despite the fact that she was talking to her new boyfriend in his car. The researcher's notes record that:

> We thought she looked better than last week. She was asking the guy in the car for a light and talking to him. After he pulled off, she explained to us that he was her 'sugar daddy' and that he drives her around the area and 'looks out' for her and makes sure that her former boyfriend, who was violent, is not about. Said she was happy 'cos she had got a place to stay – gave this as the reason she did not contact us/come to the drop in. She told us that she had stayed with this punter she'd met. He had pulled up and asked her how much she charges. She said £30. He tried bargaining with her – wanted sex for £20, she agreed £25. She said that she does not really enjoy sex with punters but this bloke was 'different'. She explained that it was because of him she was down from three to two bags of heroin a day. She said that he cooks for her – made her tuna salad and each night she'd come back to his flat 'he has a meal and a candle-lit bath' ready for her. Said she was going to finish up around 12.30 a.m. tonight and go back to his flat. She kept saying how happy she was.

Although caution should be applied in colluding with her confidence that her new boyfriend has her best interests at heart, *B* was not seen on outreach so frequently and was not spotted during the last six months of the research project. It was known that she was still around in the area with her new boyfriend. Thus it appeared that there had been a significant shift from her regular use of the street. It was not possible to follow her up to trace the longer-term outcomes of her situation. This is endemic to the nature of researching this subject area and we are left to speculate about her well-being. The point that can be confirmed is that her use of the streets as a location to sell sex (if she was still selling) had reduced over this specific time span. This was a familiar story with many of the young women, whose patterns of selling sex varied with their rapidly changing circumstances, contact with friends or boyfriends, health and well-being.

Support services on the street

Of the 21 young women regularly selling sex, 19 were contacted via outreach services that went out onto the street at night. Seventeen of the 19 made regular use of the outreach services which often included free coffee and biscuits (sometimes more substantial food), free condoms, advice on sexual health and information about local support agencies. Ten of the 21 young women had existing contact with social services departments, the remaining 11 having no contact with support workers other than through street based outreach services. Often, because of negative experiences of contact with statutory departments, including housing, social work and police, the young women had little confidence in the support services that could be offered to them. *S*, aged 18, said that it was too late now for her to use any help, noting that 'if services wanted to help, they should have helped in the past'. One young woman was particularly aware that because she was on the run from the police, it was impossible for her to approach any statutory agency for help, saying that 'social services can't do nothing for people on the run. There's nothing for wanted under age people' (*F*, age 16). She explained that she was on the run from her care home and that the police were searching for her. As she was on the run and 'wanted' she was fearful of approaching any service that may be able to offer support as she knew that they would be obliged to disclose her whereabouts. As such, in her eyes, there was 'nothing for wanted under age people'. For other young women, their own past behaviour may have discouraged workers from making undue effort to reach out and offer support, one young woman being described as 'lying, uncooperative and difficult to engage with' by a previous statutory worker.

Despite this lack of confidence, nine of the 20 young women who had serious problems with heroin use were trying to access help in cutting down on their use, four of whom were attending drop in sessions with local drug agencies – and finding this useful. As the drop in service provided regular time when workers were available each week, the facility was one that the young women knew was consistent and available. As such it was one that they used when they felt able to attend, as opposed to having to arrange appointments in advance. For example, J, aged 16, who had multiple health problems, finally agreed with the researcher that she would make an appointment to see the community drugs team and the doctor. On the day of the appointment she came to the project saying that she had been at a friend's the night before. She had drunk until 'off her head' and now had a terrible headache. She didn't feel like going to either of the appointments arranged; the researcher's notes confirm that 'K doesn't go'. Similarly, I, aged 17, explained that she 'had a meeting at AA tonight, but I'm too depressed to go and the journey takes too long'. Also, showing depression and tiredness, S, says that she 'would like to get off drugs but am too weak'. While it is inevitable that some services cannot provide a continual open door policy, the advantage of the drop in provision with its associated services 'on tap' was that young women were reassured of its availability and consistency. Making use of the drop in service was less anxiety provoking as they did not run the risk of loosing access to the resource through non-attendance. Also, if the drop in was informal, homely and holistic, the focus was not so heavily placed on the young woman's own health or social problem. This is explored further in Chapter 6.

Conclusion

This chapter has explored the reasons given by the 21 young women's case studies for starting to sell sex. It has looked at the interplay between their reported feelings of self-worth, their relationships with boyfriends, the use of drugs and the selling of sex. While noting that the majority of young women felt reticent about approaching many agencies for support, the outreach and drop in facilities available in the local areas were resources that some felt able to draw upon. Chapter 6 develops this further when considering suggestions and recommendations arising from the research.

6. Discussion and recommendations

J, aged 16

Researcher: How could friends help?

J   shoot me

[but then, looking to another young woman on the street]:

J   she looks after me and gives me condoms if I
              don't have any.

R, aged 17

Social workers should spend more time with you – keep an eye
on you emotionally, mentally.

I, aged 17

I went to the project because they help people who have
problems. They help drug addicts…they were there for me…
I used to go there and we would eat because there was a telly,
snooker and you could just go there.

Introduction

This chapter explores some of the recommendations for policy and practice arising
from analysis of young women's case studies. The quotations above reflect the
despair experienced by many of the young women, *J* feeling that the best help
offered by a friend would be for her to 'shoot me'. However, it is noted that social
work could be helpful if the young women's emotional welfare was the centre of

concern; that other young people could provide help; and that projects offering home comforts such as food and TV alongside other resources could be supportive.

Inter-agency work

Existing research and examples from practice have argued that sexually exploited young people are worked with most effectively through coordinated inter-agency work (Swann and Balding 2002, Brain and others 1998, Home Office 2000, Dodsworth 2000, Liabo and others 2000, Skidmore 2000). This involves designated members of staff from key local agencies receiving training to develop knowledge and expertise in issues involved in working with young people exploited through prostitution. To be fully effective, these staff need to be able to access resources from within their own organisations so that they can provide a coordinated 'fast track' service for young people, responding at the time of need as well as within a longer-term strategy of care. These designated staff need to be available when required, to attend inter-agency panel meetings, outlined below, regarding sexually exploited young people. Through a coordinated approach, inter-agency panels would work at a preventative level, knowing, for example, which local agency could provide a 'specialist resource', giving consistent and ongoing contact with a key-worker for the young woman concerned.

Recommendation 1
The findings from this research suggest three categories of sexual exploitation: category 1 being those at risk of sexual exploitation, category 2 being those who talk of exchanging or 'swapping' sex and category 3 being those who say they are selling sex. Responding to the needs presented in each category, it is recommended that inter-agency work between key statutory and voluntary agencies take place, initiating and coordinating local responses. The lead agency for inter-agency work will vary according to the young woman's category of risk. All agencies should refer to the work of a designated local specialist project for young people abused through sexual exploitation that provides regular and ongoing contact with a key-worker for the young woman concerned.

Category 1: Early intervention for those at risk of sexual exploitation: the role of the school

As noted from this research, early warning signs of sexual exploitation can be effectively identified by the young women's school. The research showed some cases where, having recognised early warning signs, the education authority could be effective in working with the associated problems, supporting the young woman to remain at school or to continue attendance at a pupil referral unit or other off site provision. As noted earlier, early warning signs included truancy from school, overtly sexualised and sexually provocative behaviour, sexual health problems, leaving school to get into men's cars, uncontrolled use of mobile phones and incidents of self harming, depression, excessive alcohol use and increasing drug use. Cases from this research where young women were supported to attend a group for young people who had been bullied; were received back into school despite a period of extended truancy; or were referred to a local specialist youth work project, gave examples of how these warning signs could be identified and worked with. It is evident, however, that the school cannot manage this range of service responses on its own.

Recommendation 2

It is recommended that the system in operation in Scotland, described in Lloyd, Stead and Kendrick (2001), where schools take a lead in initiating an inter-agency panel to support young people who have started to truant, be considered as a model for school led, inter-agency work with young people at risk of sexual exploitation. Sexual exploitation may be one of a range of difficulties faced by the young women. The panel's task would be to look holistically at the young person's circumstances and identify inter-agency ways to support the child. It would draw upon the services of the designated local specialist project that provided ongoing contact with a key-worker for the young women.

The devolved Scottish Executive has targeted the problem of school exclusion for specific action, aiming to reduce by a third the number of days lost through exclusion and truancy. Most education authorities in Scotland have policies designed to encourage inter-agency work to support young people in their family and their local school (Lloyd, Stead and Kendrick 2001, 1). Inter-agency school based meetings were developed in Scotland to bring together school guidance, learning support, school health, social work, community education department and relevant voluntary sector projects to consider cases of young people who had difficulty in school and were at risk of school exclusion. Central to this was, wherever possible, the attendance of the young person and their carers. With such support systems functioning, recent Scottish Executive statistics suggest lower rates of exclusion in Scotland than in England and Wales, about three times as many pupils being permanently excluded from school in England and Wales than in Scotland (Lloyd, Stead and Kendrick 2001, 10). As 42 of the 55 young women who took part in the Choice and Opportunity Project research were no longer on a school roll, and all 55 had truanted from school, an inter-agency meeting involving key service providers at an early stage would be advisable. This could provide a context for the beginning of a coordinated approach to the range of problems that they experienced. Effective inter-agency work would mean that the school, although responsible for initiating the meeting, would not be left as the sole contact for the young woman at the early stage of risk. The designated staff from the Social Services (Social Work) Department would take information to the local sub-group for children involved in prostitution (run as a sub-group, or sub-committee, to the Area Child Protection Committee as per the Department of Health Guidance *Safeguarding Children* (2000)). The Connexions service would also play a key role at this early stage of intervention. As noted in the Guidance:

> Connexions will have an important role to play in both helping prevent children from becoming involved in prostitution and in helping those already involved. Local protocols on children involved in prostitution will need to include the Connexions service. (p. 42)

Recommendation 3
It is recommended that the local protocols for safeguarding children involved in prostitution ensure that information gathered from local schools about potential risk of abuse is reported to the Area Child Protection Committee through the designated lead officer. It is also recommend that personal advisors from the Connexions service are made available to work with schools, associated education services and the local specialist project for young people abused through sexual exploitation to support young people at the early stages of risk of sexual exploitation.

Category 2: Social work led 'open door' provision for young women who are exchanging sex for favours

As noted in many of the accounts given in Chapters 3 to 5, young women who had run from home and who may be swapping sex for accommodation, money, alcohol or drugs were wary about contacting or using support offered. Frequently this was because they were fearful of the pain that could be generated by discussing their circumstances or because they thought that they would not be able to sustain a productive relationship with a service provider. They may also be struggling within a coercive relationship, with emotional and sexual attachment to one or more men who are abusing their vulnerable position, purposefully aiming to increase the young woman's isolation from service providers. Together, these dynamics mean that young women in this category can be particularly hard to identify, access and work with.

While child protection procedures and policies acknowledge emotional attachment between the perpetrators and victims of abuse, the dynamic between girlfriend and boyfriend portrayed within many of the case studies of this research suggest complex interdependence between the young woman and her abuser. While it may not be possible to physically remove the young woman from the abusive relationship, it would be possible to encourage her to consider use of injunctions, training in self defence and ongoing counselling support on self-esteem and self worth. Such work, particularly drawing on the use of peer group support and self defence training, has been developed within project work with women selling sex, and has proved to be a productive way of engaging with women experiencing violence (Blackwood and Williams 1999).

Recommendation 4
It is recommended that a dual approach be employed for work with adolescents in abusive relationships, recognising the status of adolescent as between child and adulthood. This needs to balance the interplay between both child protection and domestic violence policies and practices, aiming to incorporate the need to protect the child while providing support to empower the young woman as a developing, self-determined adult.

It has also been noted that it is the point at which a young woman may decide either to run from, or return to, care or home that they feel they have taken a decisive step – a positive step to 'do something'. It is at these points that the young woman can be supported to act in her own best interests. This demands a service informed by crisis intervention, providing a key member of staff who can track and trace the young woman's progress and who can help her begin to distinguish between short-term, emergency led provision and longer-term coping strategies. This involves the dual tasks of protecting the young person from abuse and gathering evidence to prosecute associated offending abusers. Drawing on the policies and practices developed through work under the umbrella of domestic violence, this dual approach can be facilitated by use of a range of legislation, such as the Family Law Act 1996 and The Protection from Harassment Act 1997 (see page 73). Similarly, Chapters 4 and 5 of the White Paper *Protecting the Public* (Home Office 2002) which introduces legislation against recruiting, inducing or compelling a child into commercial sexual exploitation will provide additional opportunity for prosecuting abusers. However, gathering evidence against an abuser with whom the young person is emotionally attached will continue to be fraught with difficulties. As noted in Chapter 2, difficulties exist when the young person may not want to press charges against their abuser, when their attendance and participation in the case work required may be erratic, and when they are vulnerable to further intimidation and violence as a result of bringing their situation to light. For this reason it is helpful to consider development of legislation that removes the requirement for the young person themselves to press charges against their abuser (see for example initiatives in The Netherlands: voorlichting@best-dep.minjust.nl)

Recommendation 5
It is recommended that the dual task of protecting children and gathering evidence for potential prosecution of abusers is recognised by the inter-agency sub-committee of the Area Child Protection Committee. This could be initiated by the Area Child Protection Committee sub-group for safeguarding children involved in prostitution undertaking a review of the means of gathering evidence against those grooming or coercing young people into sexual exploitation. This should be done with reference to the range of legislation that can be used to protect the child and bring a case against an abuser. The review should pay due attention to the difficulties facing young people and practitioners in gathering evidence for prosecution of an abuser, and should result in specific guidelines for practitioners and for the young people themselves in gathering evidence for prosecution.

The Department of Health Guidance *Safeguarding Children Involved in Prostitution* advocates an inter-agency approach to achieve these dual aims. It identifies key agencies that should be involved, stating that each should identify specific post holders to be key contacts within their workplace (p. 23). The Choice and Opportunity Project research suggests that despite initial goodwill, many key staff are alienated from working with some of the young women who can reject, resist or/and abuse the service. Rather than seeing rejection as an inevitable and integral part of the process of engagement, cases were invariably dropped due to poor attendance or uncooperative behaviour.

The term 'therapeutic outreach', proposed by Margaret Rosemary (one of the supervisors for the researchers), was applied within the research to explain the need for a continual open door policy by service providers. Therapeutic outreach recognises that:

- working with gaps, silences and rejection is the starting point to intervention, not the closing point;

- it is therapeutic for the young person to realise that professionals will continue to coordinate between themselves and provide a service even if the young person does not take up the offer for support at the time;

- the apparent lack of commitment demonstrated by the young person is a demonstration of distress and needs to be responded to through continued effort to reach out, rather than close down, support.

This means key staff from designated inter-agency involvement setting aside time for meetings that the young woman may not attend, or for those that may be deemed to be unsatisfactory, due to the young person's intoxication and/or extreme emotional upset. It means that time is inevitably spent networking with others who may be in touch with the young women, maintaining information-sharing that is necessary for useful inter-agency work and attempting to keep a track on the young woman's progress through joint work with others. The remainder of the working relationship may involve face to face contact with the young woman where she is able to identify or work with her problems.

Recommendation 6

When a young woman is running from care or home, involved with abusive relationships with men and coping with an escalating drug and alcohol problem, a social work care plan is coordinated by the designated social work staff of the sub-group of the ACPC for safeguarding children involved in prostitution. To maintain contact with the young women, it is recommended that 'therapeutic outreach' is used as an underlying approach to this social work service. The social work staff will need regular support from and communication with a designated specialist project for young people abused through sexual exploitation. This local project should be resourced and equipped to provide an 'open door' policy within a drop in provision capable of providing support on issues of sexual health, mental health, drug and alcohol use and domestic violence. It is particularly noted that specialist foster care provision, supported by the designated specialist project for work with young people exploited through prostitution, should be considered as a means of supporting those in need of respite accommodation whilst running from care or home.

Working with young people involved in sexual exploitation and/or prostitution can be demanding and emotionally draining.

Recommendation 7

It is recommended that a comprehensive system of staff support and regular supervision is accepted as a fundamental principle to supporting staff involved in working with young people at risk of, or involved with, sexual exploitation.

Category 3: Community safety: a partnership, inter-agency approach to enhancing safety through protecting children selling sex and prosecuting abusers

Young women selling sex on the street are at risk of violence, abuse and increasing isolation from services that can offer support. The research suggests that young women's contact with outreach services bringing advice, support and basic provisions (such as food, coffee, condoms) to the street, helps them to maintain their contact with service providers. If supported by a back up 'drop in service' providing cooking and washing facilities with support workers and advice on sexual health, drug and alcohol use and domestic violence, the outreach service can provide an essential lifeline connecting young women to essential resources. As noted, six of the eight young women who made contact via self referral were from the London Borough that had a designated specialist project, with drop in facilities, for sexually exploited young women. This NSPCC project continues to attract young women through the drop in provision, maintaining attendance over time. Although staff need to be prepared to work with a higher threshold of confidentiality than may be expected under the Children Act 1989 (see Chapter 2), contact with the Area Child Protection Committee (ACPC) sub-group for children involved in prostitution can be maintained via drop in and outreach staff. As seven of the 55 cases in the research illustrated, effective work between designated specialist projects, social services departments and the police can support a young woman to bring charges against her abusers. Also, as noted in the research findings, it was predominantly white young women who were found selling sex on the street. Asian young women who may have progressed to selling were less visible to outreach services on the street, suggesting that the sale of sex may be maintained within the 'private' domain of flats and homes. Despite this, Asian young women continued to make use of the drop in service, maintaining regular communication with project staff over the eighteen-month period of the research and then continuing to maintain contact to the present day.

At this level, the support for young people who are selling sex involves inter-agency work under the guise of 'community safety'. The Crime and Disorder Act 1998 places the responsibility for enhancing community safety on local authorities who are to undertake regular audits of crime and disorder through an inter-agency crime reduction strategy. This crime reduction strategy can advocate a range of different legislation to be used in gathering evidence against those who sexually exploit young people, those who perpetrate fear, violence, sexual and racial harassment and other offences of public disorder.

Recommendation 8

It is recommended that the Local Authority Community Safety Partnerships created under the Crime and Disorder Act 1998 take a lead in enhancing the safety and protection of young people selling sex. This inter-agency partnership must involve designated key staff from the sub-group 'safeguarding children involved in prostitution' of the local ACPC and from the designated local specialist project providing outreach and drop in facilities for young people selling sex. Other related agencies: drug and alcohol projects, sexual health and domestic violence, should be actively involved in the inter-agency work. The inter-agency group must be actively mindful of the fact that white young people may be more visible to their services, and initiate outreach and support services that aim to target black and ethnic minority young people abused through prostitution. It must also take a lead in supporting the development of treatment services for young people with problem drug and alcohol use.

Alongside the legislation identified within the Department of Health Guidance *Safeguarding Children Involved in Prostitution* – such as sections under the Children Act 1989 relating to the provision of care, accommodation, protection from abuse, abduction or significant harm (Sections 17, 20, 31, 44, 46, 47, 48, 49, 50) and the sections under the Sexual Offences Act 1956 – there is other legislation that can be used to protect children involved in prostitution. For example, legislation under the Family Law Act 1996 allows for non-molestation or occupation orders (injunctions) to be brought against those who have used, or threatened to use, violence against the applicant or a relevant child. Similarly, the Protection from Harassment Act 1997 covers conduct that causes alarm or distress to a person. Although primarily directed at stalkers, the 1997 Act makes it a crime to cause another person to feel harassed or to fear violence, the fear of harassment being enough to take a legal action, even if harassment has not taken place (Watson 1998). If proposals within the White Paper *Protecting the Public* (Home Office 2002) are endorsed in legislation, it will be possible to bring charges against those recruiting, inducing or compelling a child into commercial sexual exploitation. This range of legislation could be used imaginatively to support a young person against exploitation.

Recommendation 9

It is recommended that practitioners and young people are encouraged to understand the range of legislation that they may be able to employ against those who harass, threaten, coerce or abuse. The audits of local crime and disorder carried out through the inter-agency partnership should include proactive steps to provide support and protection to young people at risk of selling sex or involved in prostitution. This may include creating child-friendly leaflets explaining young people's right to protection and means of accessing local support.

Consistent key worker approach

The recommendations above note the need for key agencies to take responsibility for overseeing the work with young women at different times according to their circumstances. However, it is of utmost importance that young women do not experience being 'passed from pillar to post' as different agencies become involved. The young women in the research spoke of the importance of having a consistent relationship with a worker to whom they could turn at a point of crisis. They also noted the value of a 'drop in' provision where they could gain practical support such as access to food and washing facilities as well as advice on a number of different health, legal and emotional issues.

Recommendation 10

It is recommended that each local authority identify and support a designated 'specialist resource' for young people at risk of, or engaged with, sexual exploitation. This resource would provide a 'key worker' to whom the young woman could turn at various stages of their development, either when early signs of risk are identified or later if the young woman is running from home or working from the street. The staff from the resource should be actively engaged in inter-agency meetings initiated by schools, ACPC sub-committees and the Community Safety Partnerships, should take part in information-sharing under agreed protocols for confidentiality and should engage in preventative work and the delivery of awareness training throughout the local area. Examples of such projects exist through work of the major children's charities such as Barnardo's, NSPCC and The Children's Society (amongst others). These, and other models of good practice of work with marginalised and disaffected young people, should be referred to in the establishment of such a resource in local authorities where they do not currently exist.

Working with young people involved with sexual exploitation

The following diagram summarises the points made in this chapter.

Young person	Intervention	Method
Young people at risk of sexual exploitation	**Inter-agency panel initiated by school** In response to identification of young person at risk. Involving Education Welfare, Connexions, Youth Work, specialist youth projects, Social Work (ACPC sub-group for safeguarding children involved in prostitution), police, young person and carer if appropriate.	**Child centred and preventative inter-agency support plan** Risk awareness: covering truanting, running from home, drug and alcohol use, sexual exploitation and domestic violence. Child centred counselling: covering self-esteem, sexual health, physical and emotional well-being, relationship counselling. Allocation of key worker
Young people talking of exchanging sex for accommodation, money, drugs or other favours 'in kind'	**Inter-agency panel initiated by Social Service Department Lead Officer for Young People and Sexual Exploitation (ACPC sub-group for safeguarding children involved in prostitution)** Intervention plan with key worker allocation: social worker or designated support worker from specialist project service. Additional agency involvement: police, local domestic violence, drug and alcohol project and Education Social Work.	**Therapeutic outreach:** allocation of key worker, with open door policy. Supported by specialist youth project drop in facilitates. Information of respite accommodation services (specialist foster carers), sexual health services, domestic violence, drug and alcohol projects, legal services including awareness of right to protection and scope for prosecution against abusive adults. **Prevention of social exclusion:** maintaining school attendance or access to pupil referral unit or off site provision **Evidence gathering:** sharing of record keeping – incidences of being brought into police protection, dates and times of running away, intelligence-gathering of where, when and with whom running.
Young people talking of selling sex	**Inter-agency Panel initiated by Community Safety Partnerships (Crime and Disorder Act 1989)** Involving police, community safety officers, social work lead officer for young people and sexual exploitation (ACPC), specialist youth and community outreach projects, drug and alcohol projects and local domestic violence project/agency.	**Prosecution of abuser(s):** evidence-gathering against abuser(s), range of legislation to be used. **Sexual health treatment services:** via outreach services and through child-friendly sexual health clinic services. **Drug and alcohol treatment service:** working with drug and alcohol problems – focus on 'working with the problem' and on offering treatment. **Crisis intervention:** fast track service delivery targeted at provision of service at point of crisis-coordinated through the designated street based service in consultation with police and Area Child Protection Committee.

Conclusion

> In college you see a lot of young kids smiling. Why can't I be like
> that? It's about time that I put my life together. I've learnt my
> mistakes now with boys and everything. I'm not getting involved
> with a boy again. I'm going to concentrate on my studies and
> become someone someday.
>
> *(F, aged 16)*

This report has explored 55 young women's own accounts of the situations that they face through their experience of sexual exploitation and prostitution. Many of the issues raised will be equally relevant to young men for whom service delivery is likewise required.

The report proposes that the issues presented by the young women can place them in one of three categories: category 1, young women at risk of sexual exploitation; category 2, young women swapping sex for favours in kind; or category 3, young women selling sex. While these categories reflect the language used by the young people, it is important that they are understood within the context of sexual abuse and exploitation. The young women in each of these categories face a number of complex, often overwhelming, problems. Invariably, the young women are poorly equipped to respond to their own needs, struggling with low self-esteem, problems with alcohol and drug use, previous experiences of abuse and violence and current physical and mental health problems. Reaching out to contact and sustain work with the young women can be difficult for workers who may feel powerless to create productive change, rejected or abused. Despite these difficulties, case examples from the research show incidents of good practice that can be built upon and developed. These involve inter-agency work that is capable of embracing the range of needs presented by the young women through coordinated interventions between voluntary and statutory agencies.

The research findings suggest that recognition of the early warning signs of young women's risk of sexual exploitation can help to prevent future isolation from support services. Arguments for treatment services for young people who may be in damaging relationships with abusive adults, experiencing problems with drug and alcohol use and trying to cope with sexual, physical and mental health problems must not be lost. However, equal weight needs to be directed towards developing more effective preventative methods of identifying and supporting young people at risk of sexual exploitation. It is through such work that young women may feel empowered to feel that they are worth protecting, and that they can play an important role in defending themselves against abuse. As noted by *J*, aged 17:

...and you know when you get such emotion, you just feel like exploding and you just can't take no more regardless of what anyone is telling you to do, I just wanted to get out of there. That day when I finally phoned the police I felt so relieved. I would say that was definitely the happiest day of my life. I've actually done something.

Appendix 1

The Choice and Opportunity Project
The Joseph Rowntree Foundation Advisory Group

Cathy Aymer, Social Work Department, Brunel University.

Sue Blackwood, Working with Prostitutes Project, Royal South Hants Hospital, Southampton.

Dr Timothy Brain, Chief Constable, Gloucestershire Constabulary.

Pat Cawson, Head of Child Protection Research, NSPCC.

Andy Feist, Policy & Researching Crime Unit, Home Office.

Christina Galvin, Research Officer, London.

Andy Haley, Area Manager, NSPCC.

Maggie Jones, Joseph Rowntree Foundation.

Hilary Kinnell, UK Co-ordinator for European Network for HIV/STD Prevention in Prostitution (EUROPAP).

Charlie Lloyd, Principal Research Manager, Chair of Choice and Opportunity Project Advisory Group, the Joseph Rowntree Foundation.

Professor Susanne MacGregor, Director of Reseach and Postgraduate Studies, School of Health and Social Sciences, Middlesex University.

Nasima Patel, Project Manager, NSPCC.

Jenny Pearce, Choice and Opportunity Project Co-ordinator, School of Health and Social Sciences, Middlesex University.

Professor John Pitts, University of Luton.

Ian Robinson, Chief Executive, European Association for the Treatment of Addiction (E.A.T.A).

Professor Betsy Stanko, ESRC Violence Programme Director, Royal Holloway, University of London.

Dr Betsy Thom, School of Health and Social Sciences, Middlesex University.

Mary Williams, Research Officer, Northern City.

Appendix 2

Gaining credible data

As many of the 55 young women had serious problems with drug and alcohol abuse and may have been in crisis from either a recent violent attack or emotional trauma, it was difficult to rely on one-off interviews for substantive data. For example, a research officer's field notes record meeting *V*, aged 16, on the street:

> She was unwell so we put her on the tube to go home. She was unwilling to engage further but refused to be taken to a doctor or A+E. She had just been forced to have sex (she would not define it as rape) and was still recovering from her previous abortion. Little was gained from the contact about education or social work contact other than she says she 'wants to go to college and be a normal girl'.
> *(Research Officer's case notes)*

Another note records meeting *L*, aged 17:

> She got out of a car where she was in the middle of scoring from a guy; she gave us her number but was intoxicated and not keen to wait around. She had just been bitten on the arm about an hour before we met her – she asked us whether we thought she should go to A and E and get the swelling checked out.
> *(Research Officer's field notes)*

Similarly, transcripts from an interview with *H*, aged 14, show concern for the young woman who, arriving at the project after using both marijuana and heroin, noted that 'The dope wasn't really nice. I have heroin...I keep on feeling sick.' The research officer needed to support the young woman to return home to bed to rest, addressing her immediate physical needs rather than attempting an interview. When another young women, *A*, aged 14, turned up to her research meeting 'she was using marijuana and alcohol quite substantially. In fact she was too drunk when doing the first interview'. Another, *J*, aged 16, who had been selling sex on the street since the age of 13 and had a boyfriend, also her pimp

> was agitated. Has been off heroin for three days and has been
> drinking very heavily. As we sat together, she said she wanted to
> go off to score – she was going to leave to see some people for
> some gear.
> *(Research Officer's field notes)*

The implications for researching young women who are struggling with drug-related problems are explored further in Chapter 5 of this report. Here, it is important to recognise that stories presented by young women under these circumstances may either be distorted, partial, exaggerated or understandably guarded. Acknowledging this, the context of the research, the emotion behind the young women's words, and the researchers' field notes were seen as credible material for analysis as well as the actual stories presented by the young women at the time. The research drew on Holloway and Jefferson's (2000) analysis of the use of narrative where, irrespective of the actual stories told, credibility is given to the free associations made within the narrative and the context within which it occurred. Although in the examples given above the young women may not have articulated fear, pain or distress, the context of the narrative portrays these emotions.

Appendix 3

Action research in process

It was agreed that researchers should receive regular supervision from NSPCC staff and monthly consultation with a consultant from The Tavistock Clinic of The Tavistock and Portman NHS Trust. The issues raised for research officers were complex. Amongst others, they included:

- working with the personal disappointment and rejection experienced when young women broke appointments;

- understanding the impact that the research officers' own feelings, provoked through the work, had on the research process;

- dealing with the impact of hearing and working with many circumstances that were frequently distressing and sometimes harrowing.

The research methods employed, that involved engaging with individual young women over an 18-month period, tended to blur the boundaries between researcher and project worker, placing questions of researcher objectivity and subjectivity high on the agenda for analysis. In an attempt to address this, the process of doing the research was deemed to be of equal importance as the outcome. The research team worked with the hypothesis that if, during the process of the research, a young woman is helped to articulate her feelings within supported and ongoing project work, the gains of that moment are as important as those achieved in longer-term information-sharing exercises.

Bibliography

Aitchinson, P and O'Brien, R (1997) 'Redressing the balance: the legal context of child prostitution' in Barrett, D ed. Child Prostitution in Britain: dilemmas and practical responses, 32-59. The Children's Society

Alder, C and Worrall, A (2003 forthcoming) Girls Violence? State University of New York Press

Ayre, P and Barrett, D (2000) 'Young people and prostitution: an end to the beginning?' Children and Society 14, 48-59

Barnard, M, Hart, G and Church, S (2002) 'Client violence against prostitute women, working from street and off street locations: a three city comparison' http://wwwl.rhul.ac.uk/sociopolitical-science/rvp/findings/rfbarnard.DPF

Barrett, D ed. (1997) Child Prostitution in Britain: dilemmas and practical responses. The Children's Society

Barrett, D (2000) 'Young people and sex work in the Netherlands' in Barrett, D. with

Barrett, E and Mullenger, N Youth Prostitution In The New Europe, 76-94. Russell House Publishing

Behall, N and Wade, J (2000) 'Disrupted lives: how people create meaning in a chaotic world' Social Science and Medicine 50, 5, 754

Blackwood, S and Williams, K (1999) Resistance! Client-led self defence training with women sex-workers 1994-1999. Working with Prostitutes project (Southampton)

Brain, T, Duffin,T, Anderson, S and Parchment, P (1998) Child Prostitution: a report on the ACPO Guidelines and Pilot Studies in Wolverhampton and Nottinghamshire. Gloucestershire Constabulary

Broadfoot, A (1998) 'A Father's Perspective' in Ivison, I ed. Stopping the Pimp: CROP (Coalition for the removal of pimping) Conference Report. Leeds Metropolitan University, Research Paper No. 16, 29–31

Burman, M, Tisdall, K and Batchelor, S (2002) 'A view form the girls: exploring violence and violent behaviour' VRP summary findings
http://www1.rhul.ac.uk/sociopolitical-science/vrp/findings/rfburman.PDF

Calder, M (2001) 'Child Prostitution: developing effective protocols' *Child Care in Practice* 7,2, 98-115

Centrepoint (1997) *Centrepoint Annual Report 1996-1997: Getting Young People Out of Boxes.* Centrepoint

Crosby, S and Barrett, D (1999) 'Poverty, drugs and youth prostitution: a case study' *in* Marlow, A and Pearson, G *Young People, Drugs and Community Safety*, 127-134. Russell House Publishing

Cusick, L (1998) 'Female prostitution in Glasgow: drug use and occupational sector' *Addiction Research* 6, 2, 115-130

Davis, N (1997) *Dark Heart.* Chatto and Windus

Department for Education and Employment (DfEE) (2000) Statistics of Education: Permanent exclusions from maintained schools in England, Issue 10/00, The Stationary Office, *in* Osler, A, Street, C, Lall, M and Vincent, K (2002) *Not a Problem? Girls and school exclusion.* National Children's Bureau and Joseph Rowntree Foundation

Department of Health (2000) *Safeguarding Children Involved in Prostitution: Supplementary Guidance to Working Together to Safeguard Children.* Department of Health, Home Office, Department for Education and Employment, National Assembly for Wales

Dodsworth, J (2000) 'Child sexual exploitation/child prostitution', *Social Work Monographs,* 178, University of East Anglia

Firth, R (1998) 'Crown Prosecution Service perspective on pimping offences' *in* Ivison, I *Stopping the Pimp: CROP (Coalition for the removal of pimping) Conference Report* Leeds Metropolitan University, Research Paper No. 16, 29-31

Goulden, C and Sondhi, A (2001) At the margins: drug use by vulnerable young people in the 1998-99 Youth Lifestyle Survey, Home Office Research Studies 228.

Green, J (1992) *It's no game.* National Youth Agency

Green, A, Day, S and Ward, H (1999) 'Crack cocaine and prostitution in London in the 1990s' *in The Centre for Research on Drugs and Health Behaviour.* Executive Summary No. 65

Holloway, W and Jefferson, T (2000) *Doing qualitative research differently: free association, narrative and the interview method.* Sage

Home Office (2000) *Setting the Boundaries: reforming the law on Sex offences.* Home Office Communication Directorate

Home Office (2001) *Consultation on Young Runaways.* Social Exclusion Unit, CAB017658/0401/D16

Home Office (2002) *Protecting the Public.* www.protectingthepublic.homeoffice.gov.uk

Ivison, I ed. (1998) *Stopping the Pimp: CROP (Coalition for the removal of pimping) Conference Report.* Leeds Metropolitan University, Research Paper No.16, 29-31

Jarvis, T, Copeland, J and Walton, L (1998) 'Exploring the nature of the relationship between child sexual abuse and substance use among women' *Addiction* 93, 6, 865-875

Jesson, J (1993) 'Understanding adolescent female prostitution: a literature review' *British Journal of Social Work,* 23, 517-530

Kinnell, H (1999) *European Network for HIV/STD Prevention in Prostitution (EUROPAP): UK Final Report 1998-1999*

Kirby, P (1995) *A word from the street: young people who leave care and become homeless.* Centrepoint, Community Care, Reed Business Publishing

Lee, M and O'Brien, R (1995) *The game's up: redefining child prostitution.* The Children's Society

Liabo, K, Bolton, A, Copperman, J, Curtis, K, Downie, A and Palmer, T (2000) *Executive Summary: The sexual exploitation of children and young people in Lambeth, Southwark and Lewisham.* Barnardo's and Lambeth, Southwark and Lewisham Health Action Zone

Lloyd, G, Stead, J and Kendrick, A (2001) *Hanging on in there: a study of interagency work to prevent school exclusion in three local authorities.* National Children's Bureau and Joseph Rowntree Foundation

London Refuge (2002) *The London Refuge: A Safe House for Children and Young People/Annual Report 2001-2002.* NSPCC

McKeganey, N and Barnard, M (1996) *Sex work on the streets.* Open University Press

Melrose, M (2003 forthcoming) 'Labour pain: some reflections on the difficulties of researching juvenile prostitution' *International Journal of Social Science Research Methodology, Theory and Practice*

Melrose, M, Barrett, D and Brodie, I (1999) *One way street: retrospectives on Childhood prostitution.* The Children's Society

Middlegate Lodge (2002) *Middlegate.*

Noell, J, Rohde, P, Seeley, J and Ochs, L. (2001) 'Childhood sexual abuse, adolescent sexual coercion and sexually transmitted infection acquisition among homeless female adolescents, *Child Abuse and Neglect* 25, 137-148

Nolan, B, QC (1998) 'The pimp and the law' *in* Ivison, I ed. *Stopping the Pimp: CROP (Coalition for the removal of pimping) Conference Report,* Research Centre on Violence, Abuse and Gender Relations, Leeds Metropolitan University, Research Paper No. 16

O'Neill, M (1997) 'Prostitute women now' *in* Scrambler, G. and Scrambler, A *Rethinking Prostitution: purchasing sex in the 1990's,* 3-29. Routledge

O'Neill, M, Campbell, R and Webster, M, with images facilitated by Green, K, Walsall Youth Arts (2002) 'Prostitution, ethno-mimesis and participatory arts: processes and practices of inclusion in disciplines, fields and change' *Art Education: Art Therapy, Psychology and Sociology,* 3, 139-161

Osler, A, Street, C, Lall, M and Vincent, K (2002) *Not a Problem? Girls and school exclusion.* National Children's Bureau and Joseph Rowntree Foundation

Palmer, T (2001) *No son of mine!* Barnardo's

Parker, H, Measham, F and Aldridge, J (1995) *Drug Features: Changing Patterns of Drug Use amongst English Youth.* Institute for the Study of Drug Dependence

Parker, H, Aldridge, J and Measham, F (1998) *Illegal Leisure: The Normalisation of Adolescent Recreational Drug Use.* Routledge

Patel, G (1994) *The Porth Project: a study of homelessness and running away amongst vulnerable black people in Newport, Gwent.* The Children's Society

Patel, N and Pearce, JJ 'Project service delivery: targeted work with young women exploited through prostitution' *in* Melrose, M and Barrett, D (2003 forthcoming) *Young People Sexually Exploited Through Prostitution: Models of Good Practice in Britain.* Russell House Publishing

Pearce, J (2000) 'Young People and Sexual Exploitation: A European Issue' *Social Work in Europe,* 7, 3, 24-30

Pearce, J and Roach, P (1997) *Links between prostitution, drugs and violence.* SOVA publication in collaboration with Middlesex University

Pearce, J and Stanko, B (2000) 'Young women and community safety' *Youth and Policy,* 66, 1-19

Phoenix, J (1999) *Making Sense of Prostitution.* Routledge

Pitts, J (1997) 'Causes of youth prostitution, new forms of practice and political responses' *in* Barrett, D ed. *Child Prostitution in Britain: Dilemmas and Practical Responses,* 139-58. The Children's Society

Safe on the Street Research Team (1999) *Still Running: Children on the streets in the UK.* The Children's Society

Scrambler, G and Scrambler, A (1997) *Rethinking Prostitution: purchasing sex in the 1990's.* Routledge

Shaw, I and Butler, I (1998) 'Understanding young people and prostitution. A foundation for practice?' *British Journal of Social Work,* 28, 177-196

Shaw, I, Butler, I, Crowley, A and Patel, G (1996) *Paying the price: young people and prostitution.* Cardiff University School of Social and Administrative Studies

Skidmore, P (2000) *Nottingham Child Prostitution Pilot Study: Report to the Policing and Reducing Crime Unit, Research, Development and Statistics Directorate, July 1999.* London Guildhall University and The Nottingham Trent University

Stanko, B, O'Beirne, M and Zaffuto, G (2002) *Taking Stock. What do we know about interpersonal violence?* Economic and Social Research Council (ESRC) Violence Programme, Royal Holloway University of London

Swann, S and Balding, V (2002) *Safeguarding Children involved in prostitution: Guidance review.* http://www.doh.gov.uk/acpc/safeguarding childrenreview.pdf
van Meeuwen, A and Swann, S (1998) *Whose Daughter Next: Children abused through prostitution.* Barnardo's

Wade, G and Barnett, T (1999) 'Homelessness, drugs and young people' *in* Marlow, A and Pearson, G eds. (1999) *Young People, Drugs and Community Safety,* 109-118. Russell House Publishing

Ward, H, Pallecraros, A, Green, A and Day, S (2000) 'Health issues associated with increasing use of "crack" cocaine among female sex workers in London', Sex Trans Inf, 76, 292-93.

Watson, J (1998) *Domestic Violence: Guidelines for Health Professionals. Draft 5.* Camden and Islington Health Authority and Camden Multi Agency Domestic Violence Forum

Widom, KS and Kuhns, JB (1996) 'Childhood victimisation and subsequent risk for promiscuity, prostitution and teenage pregnancy. A prospective study' *American Journal of Public Health,* 86,11, 1607-1612

Woodward, K ed. (1997) *Identity and Difference: Culture, media and identities.* London: Sage
(www.drugscope.org.uk)/druginfo/d...ip\11\1\1drug_treatment_services.html

Zigman, M (1999) 'Under the law: teen prostitution in Kensington', *Critique of Anthropology,* 19, 2, 193-201

In the Beginning

When Adam and Eve gave names to all the places of the earth, they marked the beautiful downlands of Sussex for Paradise. This charming fancy, as related by the author Hilaire Belloc, serves to show why so many artists and writers have chosen Sussex as the setting for their paintings and poetry.

How many dedicated recorders of 'local colour' there are, dotted about the English countryside on warm summer days, intent on capturing, in oils or watercolours, or in memorable prose and verse, the treasured impressions of a lost time. Such poets and painters, some of whose names became synonymous with Sussex ways and byways, have made their own special mark upon the scene, in their varied attempts to discover their own version of Paradise.

Bramber is one of the most painted and photographed of the downland villages, with its imposing Norman castle keep, its ancient cottages of flint and brick, and the magnificent timber-framed pilgrim inn of St. Mary's, a house of which the writer, Ashley Courtenay, once said that 'happiness dwells in every room'. This enchanting house and its garden are enjoyed today by countless visitors who seek something of that old-world charm that remains quintessentially English.

Peter Thorogood

This Pictorial Souvenir is a companion volume to the history and guide to the rooms, *St. Mary's Bramber, A Sussex House and its Gardens* (Bramber Press).

Viscountess Wolseley at St. Mary's

from *Sussex in the Past* (1928)

At the east end of the village street there is, on the south side, an old house of some considerable size, which at once attracts attention. . . The wide paved garden, in which a piece of Florentine carved stone-work is an important feature of the foreground, enables us to step back and gain a true impression of the age and importance of the house. The heavy Horsham slabs on the roof are impressive; but what we like best are the dark-coloured beams, standing close together and set perpendicularly in the plaster-work of the walls. The beams are the strongest note and are accentuated by the creepers, which hang in festoons on the walls and are just commencing to turn scarlet, their colour being reflected in the curtains within the rooms.

St. Mary's by Garnet R. Wolseley A.R.W.A.

The house is said to have been a Cell for the occupation of four monks belonging to the Priory of Sele, and it is believed to have been the last house on the Bramber side of the old bridge that stretched across the Adur to Beeding. The foundations of this bridge were discovered in 1839, when alterations were made to the causeway that unites these two places; and it was proved by various objects then found that the Chapel of St. Mary's, also belonging to Sele Priory, stood on this bridge.

There is also, it is said, an underground passage leading to the church of St. Botolph's and some few privileged people are permitted to hear loud thuds on a doorway in St. Mary's House that is supposed to admit to this passage. These knocks are assumed to be a reminder from one of the monks who lived here long ago. . . The fact that, during the investigations made to ascertain if the passage really existed, water was admitted to the lower portion of the house, points to a possibility, I think, that this was at one time a water-way and a means of access by boat.

Although we leave St. Mary's with a feeling of bewilderment as to what does or does not date back to the time of the monk who recalls his days there and raps upon the door, we carry with us the satisfaction of knowing that the present owners look upon their possession of so lovely a place as in a sense a Trust that has been put into their hands. As time goes on and more excavations are made, as more experts give their minds to the past history of Bramber, fresh enlightenment may come in regard to this pleasant home, and this none will welcome more than the owners.

St. Mary's

A Eulogy
by Diana Durden 1988

In your quiet, low-ceilinged rooms
The leaded casements stand open
Catching in summer the scent of honeysuckle
Mingling with that old, before-time smell
Of centuries past.
Peace in such measure
Pervades a place which has seen
Guardian monks saying their offices
Pilgrims on their way to the Holy Shrine –
Your walls speak of so much
And yet give away so little.

They hug their secrets to them
While weaving that old magic
Around those who come today
Out of the twentieth-century rush
To admire your airy rooms
Gaze at your dark timbers
Delight in your dramatic past
And fall under your spell,
Promising to return again –
For you give a little of yourself
To each one to cherish for ever.

A fragment of the entrance archway c.1477 carved with bishop's mitre, Plantagenet rose and other ecclesiastical motifs.

In the old days, when St. Mary's was a monastic inn for pilgrims, this room provided accommodation for the wardens of the Great Bridge of Bramber. Towards the end of the 15th century, the Benedictine Priory of Sele, together with St. Mary's and its surrounding land, was annexed by Bishop Waynflete as part of his endowment of Magdalen College, Oxford.

13th century decorative tile, found under the floor during excavations in 1990.

The Wardens' Room

1713 to 1727
Sir Richard Gough MP
Director of the East India
Company.

Guardians of History

Some owners of St. Mary's
(with the dates of their ownership)

1727 to 1774
Sir Henry Gough MP
Supporter of Walpole.
Father of 1st Baron Calthorpe.

From c.1477
William of Waynflete
Bishop of Winchester.

The 1890s
The Hon. Gwendolen
Bourke, descendant of
Sir Hans Sloane
(a founder of the British
Museum and Chelsea
Physic Garden).

Master of Winchester College
Provost of Eton College
Lord Chancellor of England
Founder of Magdalen
College Oxford.

The 1890s
The Hon.
Algernon Bourke,
son of the Earl of Mayo,
Viceroy of India.
Owner of White's
in St. James's.

1860 to 1876
Richard Hudson
Farmer, Parish Clerk
for Bramber. He and his
wife, Harriet, had
eleven children.

1944 to 1980
Miss Dorothy Ellis (left)
with her mother. Saved St.
Mary's from demolition and
cared for the house for
35 years.

From 1984 Peter Thorogood
with Curator,
Roger Linton, restored and
re-opened St. Mary's to
the public. Key-keeper,
Bramber Castle.

The Entrance Halls

The Chapel Mystery

If it be true that '*time and chance reveal all secrets*', then one day we may discover the truth about what really lies beneath our feet as we cross the Entrance Hall to the main staircase. Since it was the custom to rebuild on existing foundations, it might be reasonable to suppose that storage space of some kind would already have existed when the present St. Mary's was built on the former Knights Templar site.

The earliest record is found in the lease granted by Magdalen College, Oxford, to Francis Shirley in 1569 for a '*Chappell house or seller*'. However, apart from a possible connection with the Sherlock Holmes story, *The Musgrave Ritual*, in which the great detective is called to an ancient house in Western Sussex only to find the butler dead in the cellar (Alfred Musgrave was owner of St. Mary's about this time), little or nothing was known on the subject until Viscountess Wolseley's reference to '*an underground passage*' in 1928. Thereafter the matter was wrapped in mystery.

Elaborate parquetry overmantel in a variety of geometrical designs, using bog-oak and possibly holly or poplar. It appears to have formed part of a larger screen at one time.

This rare, painted wall–leather was faced with silver foil, embellished with paintings of flowers and birds, tooled in a variety of patterns and finally coated with yellow varnish to give a rich, gilded effect.

About 1955, we hear of the owner of St. Mary's at the time, Miss Dorothy Ellis, having to pump out the flood-water from the cellars. Eventually she had them sealed up, and took her secret to the grave.

Since 1985, we have interviewed several visitors to St. Mary's who had memories of having played in the cellars as children. Local author, Eddie Colquhoun of Shoreham, remembered '*four rooms*', one '*like a chapel*'. In 1989, Mary Gibby, aged 88, from Philadelphia, came to see '*the chapel*' she had known as a girl in the 1930s. The poet, Anne Lewis-Smith, spent her honeymoon at St. Mary's in 1944 and remembered an '*altar*' and stone columns. Can memory play false with so many witnesses? Will '*time and chance*' finally come clean and deliver up the secret of what really lies below stairs?

A corner of the Drawing-Room showing the fielded oak panelling inset with ebony veneer.

The
Drawing Room

Immediately on entering St. Mary's, one is attracted by the warm and welcoming atmosphere that pervades every room. The wealth of panelling and marquetry throughout the house gives a pleasant air of cosiness and consequently a sense of well-being and comfort. A variety of family furniture from different periods adds to the general charm that greets us at every turn. From the Wardens' Room, or Monks' Parlour, we come into the main hall, which was once a sitting-room where the family could take coffee after lunch or dinner. There was a fine fireplace to sit round in winter and a door opened onto the garden in summer. Now the main entrance to the House, this room opens into the South Hall which leads in turn to the Drawing-Room with its fine marquetry overmantel, depicting flintlock guns, musical instruments, and a '*porcine*' bull. The canopy is supported by splendid ebonised columns. Even Teddy-bears have a place here!

Right: Peter and Mary Thorogood's Teddy-bears: the larger (1920) seated in the child's chair, the smaller (1927) plays a pretty tune when pressed!

House Party at St. Mary's
from *Free for a Blast*

Robert King-Clark, on leave from Sandhurst, recollects the halcyon days when American girls came over in the 1930s to spend their summer holidays, chaperoned by Mrs Clara Hammond of New York (a friend of the McConnels, then in residence). The young men, quite properly, settled in at the Castle Hotel nearby. . .

The next 36 hours simply flashed by. Having met the 'house party', we got down to it: we swam in the Channel at Hove; played tennis on the St. Mary's sunken grass tennis court; had tea on the lawn, drinks at the Castle under Alf Hitchener's benign gaze, and we danced in the long, low oak-beamed drawing-room of St. Mary's to such heavenly tunes as 'Stormy Weather', 'Pennies from Heaven' and 'Love is the Sweetest Thing' on the portable gramophone.

We were hooked!

…We were enchanted by the the girls' friendliness and lack of reserve to us as young men – an offshoot, no doubt, of their co-educational upbringing. We were impressed by their athleticism – they all seemed able to swim like fishes, ride like cowgirls, play tennis with style and grace, handle Canadian canoes like Red Indians and dance like fairies – and they were always laughing – at us, at themselves, at everything! They were all pretty, and dressed and groomed like shiny new pins. All the time!

The Main Staircase

Adapted from the original balustrade of the medieval open gallery which had looked over the central courtyard below, the Main Staircase leads to what were formerly domitories. These became the principal family bedrooms, now known as *The Painted Room, The King's Room*, and *The Library*. Access was also gained here to further bedrooms in the Victorian west wing which came into use for house parties. The Gallery provided handy occasional accommodation for the mysterious '*lady in grey*'!

Winter Weekends at St. Mary's

The Thorogood links with St. Mary's go back to the time of the McConnel family's residence, and Alice McConnel's friendship at Girton College, Cambridge, with her fellow-undergraduates, Hilda Sebastian and Irene Bonnett, who was a cousin of the Thorogoods of Essex, and related to the Thorowgoods of Sussex. Irene had been a pupil of the composer, Gustav Holst, and married Dr. Herbert Swann, father of the composer and entertainer, Donald Swann. Her memories of happy house parties, croquet on the lawn, and family concerts in the Music Room after dinner, remained with her into her nineties as vividly as in her younger days. Alice's other friend from university days, Hilda, wrote to us in 1985 in nostalgic mood:

I married John Gardner (printseller) in 1921 and I well remember several weekends at St. Mary's with my husband – especially in winter. We were of course – in those days – expected to appear for dinner in evening dress or dinner jackets and black tie for men. After dinner Dr. McConnel – by then an old gentlemen – liked to play Bridge. The only heat in the house was a huge log fire in the lounge! The Dr. would always wrap himself in a large warm rug and take the arm-chair back to the fire while Alice and I sat around the table freezing.

A friendly log fire still remains the most satisfying form of heating on winter days at St. Mary's. As for croquet, Irene left her croquet kit to St. Paul's Girls' School, and the old croquet lawn was ruined by the Great Storm in 1987. Our winters are still heartened by Christmas concerts with mulled wine and mince pies in The Music Room.

Newel-post candlestand.

Part of the 17th century upper staircase showing cherub newel-post.

The Gallery

Medieval 'shutting window', one of two at St. Mary's, the only known complete examples in situ in an English house. There is another in the Victoria and Albert Museum in London. The decorative panels were carved by Edwin Briar Woodford in 1912.

Victorian cast-iron oil stove in Gothic style circa 1880.

Ghostly Tales

Mysterious '*appearances*' have, from time to time, made themselves known to residents and visitors to the house in the past, though the monk who was given to knocking loudly on the door close to the South Garden has thankfully given up that irritating habit. This does not mean that '*things*' have gone unnoticed! During some revels (one imagines, fairly alcoholic) arranged by Canadian soldiers billeted at St. Mary's during the Second World War, a '*mysterious monk*' was seen wandering about in the Monks' Walk – quite a natural occupation, you would think, for such a place! At the same time we are told, '*landgirls witnessed manifestations!*' Several people have, in Viscountess Wolseley's quaint phrase, been '*privileged*' to notice the musky perfume at the foot of the stairs and outside the '*Painted Room*'. We do sometimes smell incense in the Hall. Is it a shadowy monk, fresh from Eucharist in the Chapel? Or is it just soot fallen from the chimney? Who, we wonder, was the small child in Elizabethan doublet and hose, glimpsed, however briefly, playing on the upper landing? And where has the spectral '*lady in grey*' gone, occasionally encountered by Mimi McConnel upon the stairs?

Sheelagh McConnel in 1935 standing in the place on the stairs where her grandmother used to see the ghostly 'Grey Lady'.

One of the elaborate Spanish parquetry panels in the 'Armada' doors, brought from County Mayo by the Hon. Algernon Bourke.

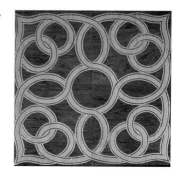

The Nonsuch Chest

Made by craftsmen working in Southwark, this architectural style of marquetry chest is associated with the domes, pinnacles and dormer windows of Henry VIII's Nonsuch Palace. The chest is one of the finest examples of this rare type of furniture and contains an intriguing secret compartment.

Created by itinerant painter-stainers in the late 16th century, the unusual *trompe l'oeil* panels of 'The Painted Room', arranged in the form of an arcade, are one of the most aesthetically satisfying experiences for the visitor to St. Mary's. Through the range of *'windows'* can be seen landscapes and seascapes, some of which are thought to be local scenes. Over the fireplace is a fine panel depicting a great sea-battle.

The Painted Room

The King's Room

The Linton family four-poster bed has no connection with the century-old legend that Charles II hid for a few hours in this room. There is a secret door, and a hiding place behind the chimney-stack used by the McConnel children and their friends to play the game of 'The King's Escape'. The tapestry panel over the fireplace depicts the landing of King Charles II on Dover beach in 1660. Thorogood and Bonnett ancestors are listed on pages of the family Bibles.

18

The Bramber Skirmish

by the Rev. John Coulton 1643

The enemy attempted Bramber Bridge, but our Carlton and Evernden with his Dragoons and horse welcomed them with drakes and musketts sending some 8 or 9 to Hell (I feare) and one trooper to Arundell Castle prisoner and one of Captain Evernden's Dragoones to Heven; all this while the enemy held the castle and a party siesed Wiston House, within a mile of Bramber Bridge.

The Flight of the King

From the account of Charles II's escape after the
Battle of Worcester by Colonel Gounter 1651

Soo wee came to Howton where on Horseback wee made a stopp at an ale–house for some bread and drinck; and there our neats–tongues stood us in very good steede, and were heartily eaten. From thence, being come to Bramber, wee found the streets full of soldiers, on both sydes of the houses, whoe unluckily, and unknown to mee, were come hither the night before to guard. But luckily (or rather, by a very speciall providence) were just then come from their guard at Bramber–bridge into the towne for refreshment. Wee came upon them unawares, and were seene before wee suspected any thing. My Lord Wilmot was readie to turne back, when I stept in and said: 'If wee doe, wee are undone, Lett us goe on boldly, and wee shall not bee suspected.' 'He saith well', said the King. I went before, he followed, and soe passed through without any hinderence.

It was then between three and fower of the clock in the afternoon. Wee went on, but had not gone farre but a new terror possessed us: the same soldiers riding after us as fast as they could. Whereupon the King gave me a hem. I slackt my pace till they were come up to mee, and by that tyme the souldiers were come, whoe rudely passed by us (being in a narrow lane), soe that wee could hardly keepe our sadles for them; but passed by without any further hurt, being some 30 or 40 in number.

The King's Escape

by Gwen Pickard 1991

A hooded form once passed this way –
A misty morn, a sunny day,
A dip of oar, a creak of wood,
Close where the flowery chestnut stood –

A warp of time. Upon the air
A glint of sword. A king's despair.
A bridge to cross – 'On with the chase!'
Soldiers shouting. A furl of lace.

'Tobacco, brandy for the warden!'
Down the tunnel through the garden –
Still we hear the footsteps so,
Walking softly, to and fro.

King Charles II

The Thomas Hood Library

Peter Thorogood's library of books and manuscripts contains the largest collection of works by the 19th century poet Thomas Hood (1799–1845). The collection includes first editions, autograph letters, comic pen-ink sketches and a unique album of watercolours.

A Reflection
When Eve upon the first of Men
The Apple press'd with specious cant
Oh what a thousand pities then
That Adam was not Adamant!

Thomas Hood (1799–1845)
(by kind permission of the
National Portrait Gallery).

Peter Thorogood
at the launch of one of his
books on Thomas Hood.

Song
There is dew for the flow'ret
And honey for the bee,
And bowers for the wild bird
And love for you and me.

There are tears for the many
And pleasures for the few;
But let the world pass on, dear,
There's love for me and you.

Educational visits: young visitors are intrigued by
the unusual collection of miniature books.

A Great Projector
Sir Frederick Trench completed the Thames Embankment *'Project'*. One of hundreds of designs for comic woodcuts by Thomas Hood. From *Thomas Hood: Poems Comic and Serious* (Bramber Press 1995)

History in a House – St. Mary's Bramber

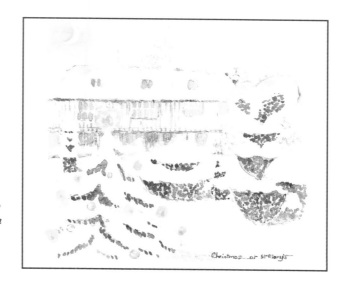

Christmas at St. Mary's. Watercolour by Daphne Allison Fisher

Like Wenceslas, with footprints strangely blessed,
Through Sussex lanes, by downland heights and coombs,
As pilgrims, then, had journeyed here to rest,
We came in snow to view the empty rooms.

Agent's prospectus clasped in frozen hand –
(No smiling welcome met us at the door!) –
We knew no reason for our anxious stand
Unless – this threshold we had known before.

Five hundred years its timbers had stood firm,
From inn to farmhouse, burgage, country seat,
Withstood the throes of war, neglect – its term
Of life but lost – beneath a builder's feet!

Once Normans, Templars, Roundheads, Ranters came –
(Memory has dimmed time's melancholy march) –
Now, thousands come to see the sturdy frame,
The dragon beam, the inglenook, the arch

Carved out with bishop's mitre, English rose;
The gilded leather, glowing in soft light;
The 'Painted Room' with fiery sea–scenes, shows
Some mystery of its past, still gives delight.

Think on these things: we stayed the errant minds
Of those who plied less positive pursuits
Than crimsom hollyhock whose seedling winds
Through unrelenting stones to build strong roots.

The years have passed, the saving has been done –
Though joys, and sadnesses, have marked our days,
Our labours less, our vision all but won–
Time–honoured house, surpassing all our praise.

Poem by
Peter Thorogood
1990

The Octagonal Dining Room richly decorated in Pre-Raphaelite style by Roger Linton, displays the splendid collection of costume dolls showing fashions from medieval to Edwardian times.

In the North Hall can be seen a fascinating display of evening bags and purses, one decorated with brightly coloured feathers, and another rare example designed by the world famous dress designer, Fortuny.

'Home is where the Heart is'

Peter Thorogood at the piano during the 70th birthday celebration concert of his music and poetry in June 1997.

In the past, owners of St. Mary's, in an effort to create a homely atmosphere, opened out rooms, put in additional ceilings to make bedrooms, installed chimneystacks, altered staircases, and added decorative panelling and marquetry, to meet not only the needs of the family in residence, but also the rapidly-changing social scene.

Frederick, 4th Baron Calthorpe, sold St, Mary's to his tenant-farmer, Richard Hudson, in 1860. The house then became at last a real family home to the Hudson children. Though some had, by then, married and moved away, great-great granddaughters, Dorothy and Mary, confirmed that they all treasured memories of those happy days spent on the farm.

Some thirty years later, a very different picture emerged with the ownership of the Hon. Algernon Bourke, who set about creating out of the ancient farm buildings an elegant family house. He added a whole west wing, complete with servants' hall, butler's pantry and still-room, additional bedrooms with attractive views of the castle ruin and quaint village street, and a nursery for his small daughter, Daphne. The most important annexe to the house was a music room with a high-vaulted ceiling. There, Algernon and his beautiful and talented wife, Gwendolen, could entertain royalty and high society to glittering *soirées musicales* in a room adorned with gilt Louis Seize furniture and a collection of magnificent early Flemish tapestries.

By 1913, the romantic and elegant age of the Bourkes was over, their treasures sold, and the McConnel family were in residence, with their jolly house-parties. So it was that, as families came and went, their beloved St. Mary's, which they regarded "as in a sense a Trust", remained ever faithful to her own time, skilfully adapting to the vicissitudes of life as history and circumstance demanded. Today, St. Mary's remains one of the most enchanting and atmospheric houses in England.

One of the most lavish extravaganzas at St. Mary's was the 'Elizabethan Feast', part of the Brighton Festival programme for the 400th anniversary of the Spanish Armada. L. to R: Peter Thorogood, actress Rosalind Shanks as Queen Elizabeth, Renée Linton, and Curator of St. Mary's, Roger Linton. The feast included an impressive 'boar's head', raised pies, salads invented in 1584, and marchpane tarts.

Concerts & Events

The Hon. Algernon Bourke's Music Room has provided author and composer, Peter Thorogood, with the perfect setting for his successful series of concerts and other entertainments. Performances have included piano recitals, song recitals, opera and operetta, literary readings, and dance. Fine actors and musicians continue to attract audiences from all over the south-east.

HRH Prince Edward in 'The Painted Room' during an informal break while filming in 1998, for his series 'Crown and Country'. Eleanor Morris and James Homer were taking part in the once popular childen's game, 'The Kings Escape'.

Below: A colourful display of 18th century dance by the Covent Garden Minuet Company.

Bottom: Dancers from the Royal Ballet receiving enthusiastic applause following their performance of the Scott Joplin ballet, 'Elite Syncopations', in a version specially arranged for St. Mary's, in 1990.

Elizabeth Jane Baldry, one of many fine recitalists to perform in the Music Room at St. Mary's.

The Gardens

Designed and planted by Roger Linton, the Topiary Garden has become a popular feature for visitors and has been included in a number of television programmes, magazine and newspaper articles.

Hollyhocks in
high summer.

View across the
Moat Pools.

From desolate beginnings in 1984, the gardens have been rescued and restored along traditional lines by Roger Linton. Besides the amusing menagerie of strange animals and birds in box and yew, he has created architectural topiary hedging in the plan of a church, with apse and transepts, all of which adjoins the mysterious cloister-like 'Monks' Walk'

Early Morning
From my Window at St. Mary's
by Renée Linton

Big tree – in the mist
Small bush – in the mist
Damp grass – in the mist
Sweet flower – 'Love-in-the-mist'
Faint hill – distant in the mist
Red sun – big in the mist
My thoughts – still deep –
In the mist of sleep.

The Lintons, through their Woolgar ancestors, have links with Sussex going back to the 14th century and with Bramber itself for nearly two hundred years. Thorogood and Linton forbears were in partnership in the 19th century through their professional association with the Honourable Company of Cordwainers.

The Victorian
'Secret Garden'
lies beyond. . .

An exceptional
example of Ginkgo
biloba, the prehistoric
'living fossil tree',
seen here in all its
golden autumnal
splendour.

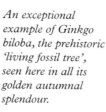

Peter Thorogood, Mary Thorogood, and Roger Linton in the South Garden.

Family and Friends

After 1945, Britain's heritage needed not so much guardians as saviours, for thousands of properties were demolished by ruthless developers. This desecration has continued, even after '*listing*' was introduced. Governments of whatever persuasion seem not to care enough.

St, Mary's owes its survival to the remarkable tenacity of one lady, Dorothy Ellis, who struggled to save the house from demolition by a local builder. What a tragedy it would have been had she not succeeded! Forty years later, St. Mary's was once again under threat and was to be closed to public view for all time, but for the courage and vision of Peter Thorogood and Roger Linton, who, together with other members of the family, pooled their resources and energies to save this important piece of our national heritage.

Renée Linton, whose warm personality and charm made her ever popular with visitors. Seen here in 1992.

Family group in 1988, includes Renée and Roger with Peter and Mary's cousin, Irene Bonnett (Mrs Swann).

A group of volunteers who have helped to keep St. Mary's open to the public over many years. L. to R.: Diana Collins, Joan Larman, Betty Thomas, Mary and Alec Holland, David Collins, Kenneth Chalmers–Dixon. 2nd row: Pam Chalmers–Dixon and Gwen Pickard.

Roger with Diana Collins at the Tudor Fayre, one of the many events organised by the Friends of St. Mary's.

Watercolour of Bramber Village by A. F. Grace c. 1880.

St. Mary's Bramber

by Diana Dykes
1993

The Adur's course had long contrived
To scant old Bramber's quay;
Town and trade no longer thrived,
Due to a changeful sea.
Sit in the garden, quiet as a mouse,
And ponder on time's wrath:
Here stood Waynflete's courtyard house
In the reign of Edward the Fourth.

The inn set out a meagre fare,
And travellers bewailed
The heavy tables all but bare,
For God and crops had failed;
And on this night you well could sight
The glint of tonsured pate:
Alarmed by Hal's dynastic plight
The monks their fate debate.

Goughs and Calthorpes came and went,
Hudsons too, and soon
The Bourkes with gardens music blent
In tones of highest noon.
Miss Ellis next deserves our thanks:
In nineteen forty-four
She slaved and saved and bullied banks
For a third of a century more.

Then Thorogoods and Lintons came –
O blessed, blessed day!
Conservers all with skills aflame
And stacks of bills to pay!
Now smoothing down her flowered gown
St. Mary's is rid of rue;
For care is the watchdog, care the crown,
And Friends have proved they do.